Bone Deep in Landscape

LITERATURE OF THE AMERICAN WEST
WILLIAM KITTREDGE, GENERAL EDITOR

Other books by Mary Clearman Blew

FICTION

Lambing Out and Other Stories (Columbia, Mo., 1977)

Runaway (Lewiston, Idaho, 1990)

NONFICTION

All but the Waltz: Essays on a Montana Family (New York, 1991)

Balsamroot: A Memoir (New York, 1994)

(Edited with Kim Barnes) *Circle of Women: An Anthology of Contemporary Western Women's Writing* (New York, 1994)

Bone Deep in Landscape

WRITING, READING, AND PLACE

Mary Clearman Blew

UNIVERSITY OF OKLAHOMA PRESS : NORMAN

Bone Deep in Landscape: Writing, Reading, and Place
is Volume 5 in the Literature of the American West series.

Library of Congress Catalogining-in-Publication Data
Blew, Mary Clearman. 1939–
  Bone deep in landscape : writing, reading, and place /
Mary Clearman Blew
    p. cm.—(Literature of the American West ; v. 5)
  Includes bibliographical references.
  ISBN 0–8061–3177–2 (cloth : alk. paper)
    1. Blew, Mary Clearman, 1939–   —Authorship. 2. American
literature—West (U.S.)—History and criticism. 3. West (U.S.)—
Intellectual life—20th century. 4. West (U.S.)—In literature.
I. Title. II. Series.
PS3552.L46Z465 1999
814'.54—dc21   99–29878
                                                                    CIP

Text Design by Ellen Beeler

1   2   3   4   5   6   7   8   9   10

For Evan and Alathea

Contents

Illustrations

Photographs are from Mary Clearman Blew's family collection.

Acknowledgments

Among many others, I wish to acknowledge the late Richard Roeder, whose interdisciplinary enthusiasm and attention to the less-traveled literary and historical trails of the West have sustained and inspired me. My cousins Tobe Hogeland Herfert and Joe Murray have generously shared what they remember of family stories. Some of the friends and colleagues who have taught and encouraged me include Kim Barnes, Bill Bevis, Alanna Kathleen Brown, Keith and Shirley Browning, Claire Davis, Carol and Ivan Doig, Steve Evans, Ladd Hamilton, Dennis Held, Ripley Schemm Hugo, Teresa Jordan, William Kittredge, William Lang, Ron McFarland, John Rember, Annick Smith, Jim and Lois Welch, and Robert Wrigley, among so many others. I wish also to express my appreciation for the example of my Idaho students, who continue to inspire me.

Although all have been revised, some of the articles and essays in this collection first appeared in the following publications, whose editors and staff I wish to acknowledge, with thanks: "The Art of Memoir" in *The True Subject: Writers on Life and Craft* (Graywolf Press, 1993); "Crossing the Great Divide" in *Talking River Review* (1999); "Wahkpa Chu'gn," *Montana Spaces* (Nick Lyon Books, 1988); "Local Legend," with a different title and very different form, in *Stories from an Open*

Country: Essays on the Yellowstone River Valley (Western Heritage Press, 1995); "The Exhausted West," with a different title and form, in *Thomas Jefferson and the Changing West* (Missouri Historical Society, 1997); "The Judith" in *Big Sky Journal* (Summer 1998); "The Daughters in Summer" in *Chronicle of Community* (1999); and portions of "Mother Lode" in the introduction to *Chip of the Flying U* (University of Nebraska Press, 1995) and the introduction to *The Curlew's Cry* (University of Nebraska Press, 1994).

Bone Deep in Landscape

The Art of Memoir

ONE OF THE OLDEST AND LOVELIEST OF QUILT patterns is the Double Wedding Ring, in which bands of colors lock and interlock in endless circles. If you want to make a Double Wedding Ring quilt, be a saver of fabric. Treasure the smallest scraps, from the maternity dress you have just sewn for your oldest daughter, from the Halloween costume you cobbled together for your youngest, from the unfaded inside hems of worn-out clothing or the cotton left over from other quilts. Keep a pair of sharp scissors on hand, and also a pattern, which I like to cut from fine sandpaper, and which will be about an inch wide by two inches long and slightly flared, like a flower petal that has been rounded off at both ends. Whenever you have a scrap of fabric, lay out your pattern on it and snip out a few more blocks.

Save your blocks in a three-pound coffee can. When the can is full, empty the blocks out on the floor and arrange them in the shape of rainbow arcs with a juxtaposition of colors and textures that pleases you. Seven pieces to an arc, seventy-two arcs to a quilt. You can sew the blocks together on a sewing machine, but I like the spell cast by hand sewing. I use a number eleven needle, an inch-long sliver of steel with an eye so fine it will barely take the quilter's thread, which measures time by growing infinitesimally shorter with each dip and draw of the needle. On my finger I wear the hundred-year-old thimble of a woman named Amelia Bunn.

When you have pieced your seventy-two arcs, you must choose a fabric to join them, in a process that is called "setting up" the quilt. Traditionally a Double Wedding Ring quilt is set up on white, but remember that you have all colors to choose from; and while choosing one color means forgoing others, remind yourself that your coffee can of pieces will fill again. There will be another quilt at the back of your mind while you are piecing, quilting, and binding this one, which perhaps you will give to one of your daughters, to trace her childhood through the pieces. Or perhaps you will give it to a friend, to speak the words the pattern spoke to you.

For years I thought of myself as a fiction writer, even during the years in northern Montana when I virtually stopped writing. But in 1987 I came to a divide. My father had died, and my husband was suffering a mental breakdown along with the progressive lung disease that eventually killed him. I was estranged from my older children. Then I lost my job. It was the job that mattered the most: I had a small child to support. And so I looked for another job and found one, teaching in a small college in Idaho, with the northern Rockies between me and the first half of my life.

Far from home and teaching again after years in higher ed administration, I felt a hollowness that writing fiction seemed to do nothing to fill. And so I started all over again, writing essays to retrieve the past—in my case, the Montana homestead frontier with its harsh ideals for men and women, its tests and its limitations. The conventions of fiction, its masks and metaphors, came to seem more and more constricting to me, like a barricade between me and the material I was writing about. But because fiction was what I knew about, I used the techniques of fiction in these essays: plot, characterization, dialogue. What I began to discover was a form that worked for my purpose.

I would select an event out of family legend and retell it in a voice that grew out of my own experience and perceptions. Often the events that beckoned to me most urgently were the ones that had been preserved in the "secret stories," elliptical and pointless and mystifying, that my grandmothers and my great-aunts told around their Sunday tables after the dishes had been washed, in hushed voices that dropped or stopped altogether at the approach of one of the men or an unwise question from an eavesdropping child. Eventually I was trusted with a few of the secret stories myself. I remember how my aunt's voice fell and her sentences became sparing when she told me a story about her mother, my grandmother. The story was about a time when my grandmother had lived alone on the homestead north of Denton, Montana, for eighteen months without seeing another woman. She had two small children and another baby on the way; her husband was away for weeks on end, trying to sell life insurance to make ends meet; and she had to carry water in a bucket from a spring a quarter of a mile from the homestead shack, which she did at twilight, when the heat of the sun was less oppressive. She began to hallucinate. She saw the shapes of women on the other side of the spring, shapes that looked like her dead mother and sister, beckoning to her. She decided she was going crazy. She had her little children to think about. They might not be found for weeks if she broke down. And so she began to go for her water in the heat of the day, when the sun scorched her trail and bleached the color out of the grass and rocks. She never saw the beckoning shapes again.

I don't understand the significance of that story for my grandmother, or why she kept it a secret except for the one time she whispered it to her younger sister in, I presume, those same stark sentences in which my aunt whispered the story just one time to me. But then, I don't fully understand why I continue to wear Amelia Bunn's thimble—it is sterling silver and engraved *AB* in a fine script—any more than I know what my great-grandmother looked like in life or as she appeared to my grandmother in the dying heat waves of that long-ago Montana twilight.

But sometimes I think I can see the turning points in the lives of dead men and women. For example, my grandmother's decision to return to schoolteaching in 1922, even though it meant breaking up her family, boarding out her oldest daughter, taking the younger children to live with her in a teacherage, leaving her husband alone on the homestead. What did that decision mean to her? I know what it means to me.

Or my aunt's mowing machine accident in June 1942, when a runaway team of sorrel horses spilled her in the path of a sickle bar that nearly cut off her foot. The disaster forced her out of the path of teaching in rural schools that she had been following and into a new life on the Olympic Peninsula. Did she understand the opportunity in the sickle bar as I do, looking back?

I feel an uneasy balance between writing about the dead as their lives "really" were and writing about them as a projection of my own experiences. I keep reminding myself that the times they lived in were not my times. Nor do the nuances of their stories necessarily reflect my assumptions about language. But unlike my grandmother, I have chosen to follow the beckoning shapes. I am who I am because of these men and women and the stories they told, and as I write about them, they live and breathe again through the umbilical tangle between character and writer.

I've been fortunate in my family's being one of storytellers and private writers who have "documented" their past. Tales, diaries, notebooks, and letters—they saved every scrap. Of course, their stories were fictions as much as mine are, told over and over again and given shape and significance. Their connection to literal truth is suspect.

For my part, I struggled for a long time with the conflicting claims of the exact truth of the story and its emotional truth as I perceived it. I restrict myself to what I "know" happened: the concrete details, the objects, the history. When I speculate, I say so.

But any story depends upon its shape. In arranging the scraps that have been passed down to me, which are to be selected, which discarded? The boundaries of creative nonfiction will always be as fluid as water.

Students in writing classes often ask, What can you decently write about other people? Whose permission do you have to ask? What can you decently reveal about yourself?

I can speak only for myself. I own my past and my present. Only I can decide whether or how to write about it. Also, I know that once I have written about the past, I will have changed it—in a sense, set it in concrete—and I will never remember it in quite the same way. The experience itself is lost; like the old Sunday storytellers who told and retold their stories until what they remembered was the tale itself, what I will remember is what I have written.

Certainly, something personal is being sacrificed, for when I write about myself, I transform myself just as I do the past. A side effect is that although the writing process itself can be painful, I experience a detachment from the finished essay because I have come to exist in it as a character, as separate from myself as any fictional character. I can read my essays to audiences with very little emotion, though once, reading Annick Smith's essay "Homestead" to a creative writing class, I began to cry and thought I would not be able to go on. Her nonfiction character moved me in a way my own could not.

Lately I have been reading my aunt's diaries, which she kept without fail for fifty years. I feel haunted by the parallels between her life and mine. She chose, perhaps with greater self-discipline, perhaps from being closer to the source of the old punishing pressures, to stay all her life on a straight and narrow path I had been perilously near to choosing for myself. Her diaries reveal her unhappiness, her gradual, unwilling resignation to her lot, and finally, in her old age, her reconciliation with the lone woman she had set out to be. Her example has left me with an enormous determination to resist those pressures and to try a new direction: having written my past, I will write the present and transform myself, as she did, in the interstices between fragment and pattern, through the endless interlocking connections between storyteller and story. I will remember that opportunity lies in the teeth of the sickle bar.

Wahkpa Chu'gn

IN HAVRE THE WIND IS CONSTANT. IT ROARS OUT OF the west over the bluffs of the Milk River, where this Montana town of about ten thousand hugs the prairie, thirty miles from the Canadian border on the brow of the continent that we northerners call the Highline. Thwarted only by the shortgrass and the shelterbelts planted by homesteaders, the wind sandblasts every exposed surface—walls, streets, faces— with stinging particles of frozen grit and snow in winter and dust in summer.

The last three years I lived in Havre were drought years, and from my office in Cowan Hall I could watch the sky to the west and see the dust storms rolling ahead of the wind, great banks of topsoil on the move. During the worst of the storms, fine layers of dust would seep in around the closed windows and rise on sill, desk, papers, everywhere, unstoppable, oppressive. It was worse than the dry years of the thirties, some of the older professors said, and I felt their apprehensiveness, their compulsion to keep an eye on the western horizon. Havre was changing. Its farming community was sinking into recession, and Northern Montana College, where I had taught for so long, had been cut back severely. There had been layoffs, and friends were leaving.

I knew by then that I would be leaving, too, and it was easy to imagine the very landscape filtering in to bury all traces of us.

The dust storms were grim enough in themselves, without arming them with imagined symbolism. The streets sometimes were so dark with dust that traffic moved with headlights, and no one walking could have cracked open an eye to see from one curb to the other. In Havre, however, no one walks. Everyone drives, even on errands of a few blocks. Havre is a town of three-quarter-ton, four-wheel-drive trucks, Blazers, Wagoneers, and Lincoln Continentals, last emblems of the glory days of oil and gas development and five-dollar-a-bushel wheat. One person per vehicle, cruising along in an upholstered steel chamber, solitary and sealed against the wind and the extremes of temperature that can range from minus fifty degrees in the winter to plus one hundred ten in the summer. Those customized windows that reflect a scenic panorama to the onlooker but which (I suppose) the concealed driver can see out of are popular.

Ironically, during the last summer I lived in Havre I went on a walking tour. I had known for years that there was a prehistoric bison kill site on the Milk River and had heard it was worth seeing, a remarkable site of its kind, unique even, but generally overlooked, like so much else on the Montana Highline that is unique. For years I had intended to visit the site, and finally, under the spur of my visiting aunt and the knowledge that my time in Havre was running out, I phoned for the times of the guided tours, loaded my aunt and my nine-year-old neighbor, Jennifer Larson, into my car, and drove west of town to the museum.

North of Highway 2, just out of Havre on the bluff over the Milk River, lies a Holiday Village mall, one of the new expansion developments of the seventies. The Village's sprawl is shrunk by the endless sky, like everything else on the Highline that rears its silhouette above the horizon, and already it looks shabby from its load of stale merchandise and from getting the

brunt of the wind, which rolls tumbleweeds and dust across its
acres of pavement. Even its colors have bleached down to the
pale, permanently windbent grasses in the borrow pits and the
ochres of gravel. And across from the Village, south of the highway, lie the equally windswept and faded Hill County fair-
grounds, a public park where tourists can camp overnight inside
a small shelterbelt of Russian olives and caraganas on irrigated
green grass, and the Clack Museum.

On the Highline, the summer evenings seem to go on forever, and at seven this evening, when I park outside the museum
with my aunt and Jennifer, the sun is still high and brilliant, and
the air is heavy. The wind has subsided, as it sometimes does in
the late day, but it rags at the weeds and whines off the white
siding on the museum. Bicyclists and campers with trailers are
beginning to turn into the park and stake their claims, setting
up their tiny, transitory community of strangers for the night.
Outside the front door of the museum, obviously waiting for
something to happen, stands a small group of people.

Jennifer and my aunt and I get out of the car and wait with
them: a young, tanned couple who look skeptical at what clearly
seems an amateurish, poorly organized little event, two middle-
aged couples with cameras, and a young man with a vacation
beard. Jennifer and I are the only locals. Even my Montana-born
aunt has lived out of state for years.

A few minutes pass. Jennifer, indifferent to adult embarrass-
ments, wanders over to a rack and begins a comprehensive selection from its free pamphlets and brochures. My aunt, the only
one present to reveal any delight or anticipation, waits with her
hands clasped behind her back and her eyes sparkling. Then the
screen door opens and bangs shut, and down the steps bounds
Elinor Clack.

Elinor is about four feet ten, dressed in blue jeans and a
jacket, with short gray curls and bright blue eyes. Although she
and I have been acquainted for years, she gives me no special
sign of recognition as she counts us; she is being professional,

and we all feel better for it. Despite her shortness and her late-
ness, Elinor is a stiffening breeze. Nothing under her charge
could possibly be slipshod or half-hearted or embarrassing, and
we gather around her.

"Okay," she says, briskly. "Back in your cars. We meet down
by the entrance gate to the jump site. Anybody want to ride
with me?"

The bearded young man accepts her offer. He is a bicyclist,
traveling by himself. Elinor gives directions to the rest of us: we
are to head back east on Highway 2 as far as the city water plant,
turn north and then west on a dirt road we will find deliberately
unmaintained, and follow it for a quarter of a mile until it ends
at the jump site, just under the bluff from the shopping mall.

Jennifer and my aunt and I climb back in my car and follow
Elinor's small convoy back down the hill toward Havre, past the
water plant, and west along the Burlington Northern tracks and
the river. Jennifer and my aunt lean forward in their seats. They
can hardly wait, they are eager for whatever is to be seen, but I
keep my eyes on the road, which indeed is badly rutted from the
last rainstorm, months and months ago. Below us coils the river,
shrunken back from its banks and sandbars by irrigation pumps
and drought, and above us looms the bluff.

We are last in line, and by the time I have pulled over on the
grassy knoll and parked, the others are out of their cars and hik-
ing up the path to the chain-link fence. Elinor is unlocking a
massive padlock.

"Vandals," she explains. "We have a terrible problem with
vandalism. That's why I don't keep that road maintained."

Here under the bluff the wind loses its force, and the air is
still and warm. Sounds are muted. There might not be a highway above us, or a shopping mall, only sky and the cutbank,
overgrown with grass. Mica sparkles, the river sparkles. For a
breath, in the small sounds of shoes crunching on shale and the
snapping of grasshoppers, in the smell of river mud and ripe
grass and sagebrush, I am back in the Montana of my child-

hood, with real earth under my feet and real sky over my head. If anything in my experience seems permanent, it is the prairie, with its pale turn of seasons, the quiet cycle of the grasses, the shadows of the clouds; and for a stabbing moment I wonder how I can leave it. I look to see if anyone else has felt its summons, but everyone has followed Elinor up the ruts that lead to the first house. Even the skeptical young couple is listening to her commentary.

The Wahkpa Chu'gn site derives its name from the traditional Assiniboine name for the Milk River: the "middle" river, between the Missouri and the Bow. The site is fenced in chain link and stretches over a few hundred yards between the bluff and the river. All that can be seen, except for a glimpse of the roof of the shopping mall and the tops of its green dumpsters at the crest of the bluff, is grass and fencing and the houses. Literally, houses, painted white, with eaves and windows, about twelve feet wide by sixteen long. They remind me of the old house on my grandmother's homestead.

Anywhere else—just across the border at Fort Walsh in Alberta, Canada, for example, or along the tourist trails in southern Montana—there would have been a plan and organization to bring this site under control, with strategies to market it skillfully. Structures and facilities would have been designed and decorated. Nothing stark or shabby would have been an embarrassment for young couples from the East on their way to the West Coast.

But not here, not on the indifferent Highline. The small structures that shelter the exhibits were built by Elinor Clack's own hands, and by the hands of members of the Milk River Archaeological Society, which describes itself as "a serious group of amateur archaeologists." These serious people paid for most of the materials themselves and built what they knew how to build: houses.

In fact, the site today looks much as it would have looked two thousand years ago when prehistoric Indian hunters first drove bison over the bluff to be killed and butchered. Elinor says that, over the two-thousand-year span, erosion has blunted the angle of the bluff and deposited new soil over the buffalo bones, raising the floor of the coulee as much as twenty feet from its prehistoric level. Certainly in comparison with museum panoramas I have seen that depict sheer hundred-foot cliffs with tiny dark plasticine figures suspended head over tail in midair, this drop seems undramatic. Inadequate, even. Would it really kill a buffalo to drive him over this bluff? I could easily ride up it, or down, on horseback, and I see doubts on other faces. But allow for the erosion, says Elinor, and then consider the evidence of a corral structure in the upper Exhibit A area. The prehistoric hunters would have counted on the corral at the base of the bluff to hold stunned or injured buffaloes until they could kill them with arrows. Nothing dramatic about it, just bloody day-to-day living.

Elinor unlocks the door of the lower house and we all file into a dim stifling room of raw joists and stand around the oblong pit, like a cellar hole, in its center. The pit smells musty and overused, like a cellar, and its floor is littered with fragments of bone that drain away talk. As my eyes adjust to the dusty light from the window in the eaves, I see that bone fragments protrude from the walls of the pit—that in fact we have been walking all along on a mound of bones.

"This pit exposes cultural layers from three archaeological phases," explains Elinor. "The deepest bone layers represent the Besant phase. Radiocarbon analysis establishes the earliest Besant use of Wahkpa Chu'gn at 50 B.C. Evidence from other bison kill sites indicates it was at that time—two thousand years ago—that prehistoric hunters of the northern plains developed the bonds and skills needed for communal hunting."

Everyone stands in silence around the charnel. Jennifer, who soaks up all knowledge, takes careful notes in her school tablet. Then we all file out behind Elinor and follow her up the grassy slope to the next exhibit.

The next house is built into the side of the bluff. Under its eaves the earth has been pared away to expose the faint layers of dun and gray and ochre that mark the succession of cultures buried under our feet. Elinor points out a faint black ring.

"Fire," she explains. "The lower exhibits were kill sites, but this was a campsite. Up here, under the eaves, we've excavated a fire hearth. Would anyone like to climb up and take a look?"

A pause. The steps look precarious, the location of the hearth dusty and obscure under the eaves. Some of the women are drawing back. One wipes her perspiring face with a tissue.

"Oh, yes, I would!"

My aunt dodges out of her place in line and climbs cautiously up the ladder. We all watch her wrinkled face under her mop of white hair as she peers into the excavation. She hangs up there for the space of several breaths, as intent as if she can smell the smoke of the cooking fires, before she climbs back down. Jennifer is right behind her to take the next turn.

"How old did you say that hearth was?"

"About a thousand years old."

Now, of course, we all climb up to take a look. When it is my turn, I stand on the wobbling step and look into a scraped-out hollow of earth in the stifling heat under the eaves. Plainly it has been blackened by fire, as though yesterday, except for the absence of dead embers. Gradually I understand my aunt's intensity. It is as if, perhaps in one more breath, or in the breath after that, I will catch a whiff of charred wood and cooked meat and even of the steadily working hands that feed the fire and drop the heated stones into the skin water pot. The thousand years elude me—all I can really smell is packed and desiccated earth—but the sense remains that the smoke is there, pungent, drifting, just beyond my perception. Elinor, watching me from the sunlit doorway, smiles.

"Whew!" says one of the men, mopping his face once we are outside again.

"Imagine what it must have been like a thousand years ago,"

says Elinor. "Alone, about this time in the evening, with the sun going down and the smoke rising from the fires—"

"And the flies! And can you imagine the smell?" the man interrupts. "It would have been like a slaughter yard. A slaughter yard is what it was."

"Yes. It was a slaughter yard and a meat-processing plant. The hunters came here to kill buffalo and make pemmican. Some of them lived here permanently. Evidence from buffalo fetal bones shows constant human occupancy, particularly through the winter."

It would have been familiar. Home. Season after season, setting the children and the old people to kindle fires and prepare for the bison drives, a cycle broken only by death. Our knowledge of what it would have been like to live in such permanence is as elusive as the vanished smoke.

"Across the river," says Elinor, "may have been their burial places. The river was wider then, and shallower—you can see the marks of the prehistoric channel—and they could have waded across it."

We all look across the mile of river bottom, dotted with cottonwoods and patched with fields of irrigated alfalfa. The line of bluffs to the north is bare and bleached, unaltered since the retreat of the glaciers and no more remote than those Besant or Avonlea women butchering meat or tending their fires while their children hunted for berries along the coulee. Their two thousand years, after all, reduces Havre's time here to a shrug.

"How did this site ever come to light again?" asks the bearded young man.

"A schoolboy named John Brumley found it in 1961. He had heard a local story about how the crews had dug through tons of bones when they were building the railroad, and so he rode out here on his bicycle and looked. Later he watched the archaeologists and worked beside them and became expert himself."

There remain the actual kill sites to be viewed. Elinor leads us farther up the coulee to the exhibit houses at the base of the drop. By now we are prepared for the close air and stifling heat, the dim light over the excavation pit, the encrustation of bones in the earth walls. But the kill sites elicit several drawn breaths. Even knowing what to expect, who could have dreamed of so many bones? Bones, tons of bones, fragments of bones in endless chaotic patterns, embroidering the layers of sifted dust and earth washed down from the coulee walls, bones, bones deeper than we are tall.

Elinor explains how, over a period of several days, the hunters drove the buffaloes from the high plains around the buttes, hazing them into drive lanes of stones and piled-up brush that gradually narrowed as they neared the bluff. Then, at the chosen moment, an uproar from the hunters, yelling, waving buffalo robes, making noise, stampeding the enormous animals into a panicky gallop over the brink.

She shows us the traces of post holes, two or three feet apart, that outline the circular corral at the base of the drop. Each post hole once contained two upright posts, wedged in place by ceremonial buffalo skulls. One of these skulls remains in the pit, intact, somehow surviving the years of neglect after the coming of horses to the Plains Indians revolutionized their hunting and made the buffalo jumps obsolete. Then the years of erosion, the damage done by the building of the railroad, and finally the vandals.

"Vandals," says Elinor, locking each heavy door carefully behind us. "I don't know how many windows and doors I've had to replace."

"Looking for souvenirs?" guesses one of the men.

"Well—yes. More than that, they seem bent on destruction. A few years ago, I found this door kicked in. The panel broken. That evening I came back with a piece of plywood and a hammer to repair it, and someone shot at me."

In silence we walk back down the slope to the parked cars. The sun is low now, and briefly the grasses are golden. The wind has relented, and the river holds what is left of its channel and reflects sky and clouds and the tops of the cottonwoods. No one says a word. It is still hot, and the hike has been fatiguing, up and down the steep slope. Then too, the site imposes its own burden. Something here is as oppressive in its own way as the successive layers of earth and bone. After all these years, some spirit is still powerful enough to want destruction, even to the point of someone's firing shots at the guardian of the place, Elinor.

On the drive back to the museum, Jennifer reads through her collection of pamphlets. Being Jennifer, by now she probably can tell a Besant-phase arrowhead from an Avonlea, or one from the Old Woman phase. Her lips move silently as she reads, her face is beaded with perspiration and new freckles. I wonder what she will carry away of Wahkpa Chu'gn. Apparently it altered the whole course of John Brumley's life.

Next to the Clack Museum stands a restored homestead house—a small frame house, painted brown, not unlike the exhibit houses under the bluff and certainly no bigger. None of the relics it contains can be dated much earlier than 1910, when most of the Highline was homesteaded. The Highline had been one of the last northern plains regions where remnant Indian populations were pushed off into starvation and death by disease to make way for white settlement, in a time within living memory, both Indian and white.

But apparently these homestead relics are worth stealing or smashing, because the door is locked. The young couple shade the glare of the late sun with their hands to peer in at a window.

"What is that tub with the handle for?" the woman is asking.

"I don't know. Maybe a churn?"

My aunt stops short. "Oh, no! That's no churn! It's a washing machine!"

In the face of their surprise, she plows on. "My mother had one like it. I remember it perfectly well. You carried water from the boiler on the wood stove to fill it. Then you put the clothes and the soap flakes in, and you pulled back and forth on that handle"—she points out the handle on the tub, the one that suggested a churn—"until your clothes were agitated. Then you wrung them out and rinsed them, and wrung them out again and hung them out to dry. You drained the water out of your washing machine through a plug in the bottom."

They are staring at her as if she's just stepped out of, say, the early Besant period.

"A lot of backbreaking work," the young man murmurs at last.

Something lives on the Highline that cannot examine itself. Outsiders recognize its presence but fail to describe it, hurrying instead over the prairie highways at eighty miles an hour to reach the more conventionally spectacular scenery of the mountains.

Judging from the closed and sullen faces in the old photographs in the museum, the hysterical invective rising from the pages of the earliest newspapers, it has existed here since the first white exploration and settlement of the Highline. Perhaps it is the quality that perpetrated genocide, or perhaps it is the inevitable outcome of genocide, a kind of mark of Cain.

Whichever it is, it endures, excluding the outside world and yet failing to settle here, failing to call it home. Rather than admit it has a past—and therefore guilt—and mortality, it shuts itself away in indifference or drunkenness or chauvinism, keeping to itself even among others of its own kind, but ready to lash out on any provocation or hint of a threat. The record of its own past is a threat, and Wahkpa Chu'gn is just such a record—of the roots it cannot claim, of the fate it cannot accept.

To live in Havre is to live in a dilemma. Introspection is subversive here, and memory treasonable. And yet it is the brink on which we all live, the blade of the knife pressed against tomorrow. In Havre the wind is constant, but two thousand years are as close as yesterday, and we cannot keep ourselves from looking back.

Crossing the Great Divide

It's gone away in yesterday.
Now I find myself on the mountainside
Where the rivers change direction
Across the great divide.
　　　—KATE WOLF, *"ACROSS THE GREAT DIVIDE"*

I PLAYED MY PART IN THE WESTWARD MOVEMENT A century after it was supposed to have ended. I was no longer a girl, and I wasn't laughing, I was close to tears. With a hundred boxes of books and some household furniture loaded into a borrowed horse trailer and the back of a pickup truck driven by my brother-in-law, with my youngest child, Rachel, who was not yet five, and two sedated cats in the car with me, I drove out of Montana, where I had lived the first half of my life, and crossed the divide into Idaho.

It was the summer of 1987, just six years short of a century since the founding father of western history, Frederick Jackson Turner, in his famous 1893 address, "The Significance of the Frontier in American History," had drawn down the curtain on the frontier, which he defined as "the meeting point between savagery and civilization." After 1890, Turner noted, no vast

tracts of land remained on the North American continent for
expansion and conquest, and therefore the primal agon, the pioneer struggle with the wilderness that for four hundred years
had restaged itself farther and farther to the west, the experience
that Turner believed had honed European immigrants into
Americans, had come to a close.

I was not thinking about Frederick Jackson Turner as I
drove up to the Lolo summit that July of 1987. As I passed the
rainbow sign that told me I was leaving the Big Sky Country,
passed the grassy clearing with the public toilets and the tourist
information booth in the shade of pines, passed the truckers
resting their rigs and checking their brakes before beginning
their long grind down the other side, all I had on my mind was
reaching the crest of the divide and entering strange territory.
Strange colors on the license plates that bore the "Famous
Potatoes" label of Idaho, unfamiliar designs on the state highway
trucks and heavy equipment. Beyond the purplish "Welcome to
Idaho" sign, I could expect the grade to be steep and downhill
and, as the next sign warned, narrow and winding and without
services for another eighty miles.

On the other hand, now that I had crossed the state line, I
could breathe freely again. I was safe, or safer, at least. Troopers
from the Montana Highway Patrol wouldn't be signaling me to
pull over, wouldn't be serving papers filed by my husband to
keep me from taking our daughter out of the state. The fact was
that, like so many of Turner's frontiersmen, I was as much running from something as headed somewhere.

My husband, whom I had loved, was adventure gone sour.
It wasn't that I had been a girl spinning a dance with her own
shadow when I met him. I was a grown woman with two children, and I already had been working for years at the small state
college in Havre, on the Montana Highline, when he waltzed
into my bookish life with his disdain for conventions, schedules,
deadlines. At eighteen he had left the ranch in Kansas where he
had grown up. He had worked as a roughneck in the Oklahoma

oil fields, run mud trucks in Colorado, operated a drilling rig in Wyoming. In the boom-bust culture of the oil patch, he made money, spent money, lost money. Broke, he came to northern Montana and made a small fortune scalping oilfield pipe. Bought an airplane and courted me.

When Rachel was born, he was already beginning to show the effects of the degenerative lung disease that eventually would kill him—his fingernails clubbing and turning dark blue, his shortness of breath, his inability to concentrate. He refused to believe that he was ill. Insisted that he wasn't losing money. Another cast of the dice, another spin, and he knew he would dance back to the top. But the next cast of the dice was bankruptcy, and the next spin was the downward spiral of pulmonary fibrosis. Weight loss, paranoia. He became abusive.

Don't try to leave me, Mary, or I'll make sure you'll never see that little girl again, he warned.

How seriously could I take his threat? How could I not take it seriously? I had a restraining order against him, but I knew he was driving around the neighborhood, watching my house, and I had nightmarish visions of his snatching Rachel into his car and heading for Kansas with her. Meanwhile my job at the college in Havre would end with the fiscal year. I was due to start teaching in Idaho in the fall. What if he tried to stop me? Could he keep me from taking Rachel with me?

As we worked into the night, stowing boxes and furniture into the horse trailer, my sister and I devised a contingency plan for spiriting Rachel and me out of town in a friend's car at the first sighting of anyone who looked as though he might be serving the papers for a restraining order on me. None had, we hadn't had to use the plan. And now I had crossed the divide, and I was driving into Idaho on a winding road, with everything I owned ahead of me in my brother-in-law's truck and the trailer.

The altitude at the top of Lolo Pass is almost exactly a mile. Heading west, Highway 12 rises steeply to crest the Bitterroot Range, which rears its peaks and sprawls its almost impenetrable ridges and ravines on both sides of the long and twisting boundary between Montana and Idaho. From the crest, the highway drops almost as steeply into the gorges carved out of the mountains by the Lochsa and the North Fork of the Clearwater River and eventually emerges at the confluence of the Clearwater and the Snake, where the bluffs stretch their dry, bare shoulders into the Columbia Plateau.

When I dared to take my eyes off the hairpin turns of Highway 12, I could look off the verge of the asphalt into some of the most spectacular scenery in the world, and some of the most historic in the Rocky Mountain West. White pines and cedar bristled up the steep sides of ridges, and boulders the size of houses broke the sheer drop-offs into ravine after ravine that faded beyond eyesight into wave after wave of mountain peaks as remote as clouds and capped with snow even well into July. The air smelled of balsam fir and warm grass and diesel. I kept telling myself I had no reason to cry.

Without knowing their names, I was seeing the highest peaks of the Bitterroot Range. Grave Peak, 8,270 feet. Rhodes Peak, 7,950 feet. McConnell Mountain, 7,415 feet. And in those peaks and ridges that seemed to roll forever toward the west until they merged into the hazy blue of the atmosphere, I was seeing what Meriwether Lewis had seen when, over on Lemhi Pass in August 1805, he and three of his men had split from the main body of the Corp of Discovery and followed an Indian trail to a point where no white men had stood before and looked out at "immence ranges of high mountains still to the West of us with their tops still partially covered with snow."

If Meriwether Lewis felt surprised and discouraged at what he saw, looking west from Lemhi Pass, he had good reason. He was not seeing what he had expected. Eighteenth-century geographers had, after all, posited a kind of through-the-looking-glass theory of the unknown North American landscape. Supported by one or two reports from European explorers and the scant information that had been gleaned from Indians, Thomas Jefferson, for one, believed that the unknown might be mirrored by the known—that the mountain ranges and river drainage systems of the western side of the continent might replicate, on a larger scale, those on the eastern side. On the theory of landscape as symmetry, Lewis and Clark had hoped that from the summit of the great divide they would discover on the western slopes a mirror image of the eastern slopes and, most vitally for their charge from President Jefferson to discover an easily navigable water route to the Pacific, they would find, flowing into the Columbia, a drainage system that duplicated the Missouri River drainage system to the east.

I can imagine a certain comfort to be drawn from the concept of landscape as a hall of mirrors—predictability, and all the aesthetic pleasures of design, with the reassurance of order, like a spun web between us and the boiling chaos of the cosmos. But then I imagine the theory being applied to the cosmos, imagine applying it to time as well as space. On the one hand, a promise of the familiar in the unfamiliar, but on the other, the terror of a stasis so complete that any door in any corridor leads to the same corridor, that any choice will have the same outcome as any other choice. Circular, dizzying, a maze leading everywhere and nowhere. I think chaos theory finally may be more comforting than symmetry theory.

Not that Lewis and Clark would have envisioned the territory west of the continental divide as a garden of forking paths. Their theory of symmetry in landscape was more down to earth, less fearful in its implications. They wouldn't have expected every creek and clump of sagebrush on the eastern front to be duplicated exactly in the west, and even if they had, the hundreds of strange species of wildlife and vegetation that they had catalogued thus far on their journey would have disabused them of such a literal application of symmetry theory by the time they got to the summit. No, Lewis merely wanted to believe, that day on the crest of the North American continent, that the worst of the Corps of Discovery's ordeal was behind—that it would be downhill from here on, and he and Clark and the others would travel by canoe, with easy portages, the rest of the way to the Pacific. That they would return to Jefferson with confirmation of his hopes for an artery of rivers connecting the two rims of America, and that history would get on with itself. That they themselves would become wealthy and famous.

If Lewis had an inkling that the wilderness he saw from the summit of Lemhi Pass was, in its absence of symmetry, a hell in which he would eventually lose his bearings, he never said so in his journal. "I felt perfectly satisfyed," he wrote, "that if the Indians could pass these mountains with their women and Children, that we could also pass them."

What lay ahead for him and Clark and the rest of the Corps of Discovery, however, was misery beyond their reckoning as they made their way through the western ranges of the Bitterroots in the freezing rain and snow of September to what is now the Lochsa River but in 1805 was the Kooskooskee. With their packhorses starving for lack of grass, with their own provisions exhausted, they killed the colts, shot a few grouse and a coyote, and caught crayfish to survive for a desperate eleven days while they traveled 160 miles of sheer rocks and fallen timber and rapidly accumulating snow until they reached the shelter and succor of a Nez Perce village.

And if Lewis is never explicit in describing his response to the west front of the mountains, his journals and Clark's undergo a radical shift in tone as the men describe their progress down the Lolo Trail, as they attempt the magnificent, terrifying rivers of Idaho—the Salmon, the Clearwater, the Snake—and finally as they survive the rapids and portages of the Columbia, with the reverberating names—the Celilo Falls, the Long Narrows—only to find themselves alive, ragged, and battered by the alien rains and bitter winds of the Pacific coast. "The winds violent trees falling in every derection, whorl winds, with gusts of rain hail and thunder, this kind of weather lasted all day, cer-

tainly one of the worst days that every was!" wrote Clark.
Whether from sheer misery, from a genetic tendency toward
"melancholy," or from the effects of the landscape itself, Lewis
began a descent into depression that, in spite of the success of
the Corps of Discovery and all the accolades, would lead him to
financial and political ruin and death, probably by suicide,
within three years of his return to the United States.

As the silhouetted figures of Lewis and Clark on the historical
markers are a constant reminder, today's Highway 12 approxi-
mately follows the old Lolo Trail that the Corps of Discovery
struggled down in September 1805, the same trail that the Nez
Perce Indians previously had used for centuries to cross over to
the east slopes of the Bitterroots on their annual buffalo hunts.
Down from the summit, in the shadows of vertical cliffs where
the white pines hang on by their roots and boulders leave trails
of gravel when they crash down and roll across the asphalt,
Highway 12 meets the Lochsa River and follows it for another
seventy hairpin miles through the Selway-Bitterroot Wilderness
to the tiny mountain hamlet of Lowell, Idaho, where the Selway
River joins the Lochsa, and then to the little town of Kooskia—
pronounced Koos-Kee, after the old Kooskooskee—on the Nez
Perce Indian reservation, where the Selway and the Lochsa converge with the South Fork of the Clearwater. Highway 12 has
been a modern, paved highway only recently; until 1962, it was a
graveled trail over the mountains to be attempted by the truly
daring.
      Since the first time I crossed the divide in July 1987, I have
driven Highway 12 over Lolo Pass some twenty or thirty times, at
all seasons and road conditions. On the Memorial Day weekend
of 1988, I was on the way home from Missoula, Montana, in a
blizzard of wet snow. Rachel was with me on that trip, too. She
cheered the snow from the back seat, planning the snowman she
would build when she got home, while I fought our way over
Lolo in zero visibility with the windshield wipers accumulating

clumps and gobs of snow and ice that I had to stop and break off by hand. But on the Idaho side, we drove into a warm rain that gradually cleared as we descended into the river gorges, and I remember the relief I felt, and Rachel's disappointment over her snowman.

In January 1989, on my way to a conference over in Montana, I drove over Lolo Pass on solid ice that seemed to slide and shift under my studded snow tires. My car would veer toward the trucks skidding their own way down the pass in the other lane, then veer toward the frozen river a hundred feet below the highway. After miles on that unforgiving ice, my fingers were cramped in the shape of the steering wheel and my back and shoulders rigid with a tension that I can still feel when I am reminded of it.

During the terrible summer of drought, when Yellowstone Park burned into an inferno, wildfires broke out in Montana and Idaho and hotshot crews from all over the west converged on meadows where Lewis and Clark had camped. They were fighting the fires through the same impasses of tinder-dry deadfall, into the same barricades of brittle lodgepole pine, over the same treacherous slides of scree. Smoke hung over the pass that summer, the blackened skeletons of firs smoldered on slopes that had burned right down to the highway, and flames danced the ridges within sight of my car window. At one point, I waited in a line of traffic that had been held up while a helicopter eased down with a giant bucket, dipped water out of the Clearwater, and whirled it away to douse one of the fires.

My worst crossing was in July 1990, when I was driving my aunt back from the last visit she ever made to Montana, and, seventy miles above Lowell and the nearest services, she began to hallucinate. Rachel was riding in the back seat. It was a beautiful summer of deep grass and wildflowers along the highway, dark red paintbrush and paler mountain geranium. Above us, Stellar's jays flashed blue through the dark green pines and eagles floated against endless clouds. Below us, the Lochsa foamed and

tumbled its whitewater rapids and tossed loads of rafters whose
screams of delight carried all the way up to the car—and my
aunt, disoriented, wondered who lived in all the houses she
thought she saw from the car window. I still feel sickened when
I remember that drive.

Lolo Pass does hold its rewards. One late afternoon in
summer, just over the line into Montana, I braked as a young
moose reared out of the underbrush and clattered across the
highway in front of my car. Its ungainliness in human eyes—
the big, lumpy head, the disproportionately long legs—was bal-
anced by its indifference. It lived in its own bubble of
experience, and, as it disappeared in timber, it never glanced at
me in mine.

And just last September, driving home from Montana in the
rain, I took my eyes off the wet highway for a few seconds and
saw, belly deep in the river, the Selway elk herd. Perhaps twenty
big, self-contained bodies, yellow-rumped, necks gracefully low-
ered as they drank from the river. I was able to glance back just
once as the highway curved. The sun had broken through the
rain clouds, and one shaft illuminated the elk in the dark green
water, and then I was another mile down the road.

I had been graced with the beauty of the remembered
moment. The sodden cedars and firs that crowded the opposite
slope and reflected their dark and fractured density in the river
current; the sunlight that broke through the purpled, jangling
rain clouds and gilded the backs and rumps of the elk. But if I
had had a vision of Eden, it was an Eden of forking paths that
would never converge. I had seen the elk through my car window, after all; I was a human with my nose pressed against the
glass, straining for a glimpse into the parallel universe of creatures that would return my gaze only with indifference or with
fear.

After I had lived in Idaho for a few years and learned some of
the local history, I understood more of the terrors of the divide.

Before I left Montana, I had read Andrew Garcia's *Tough Trip through Paradise*, his account of following the old Indian trail on horseback over the mountains in 1878 with his teenaged Nez Perce wife, In Who Lise. In Who Lise had crossed the divide from the other direction the year before, when she and other members of Chief Joseph's band of nontreaty Nez Perce had defied General Howard's order to return to their reservation. The Nez Perce had fled east into Montana with the troopers chasing them, over the precarious ridges, the boulders and ravines and wind-fallen timber and rockslides. When the troops caught up with them at the Big Hole and mounted a dawn attack on the sleeping camp, In Who Lise had been wounded and her father killed in the warriors' desperate defense and counterattack, which had allowed most of the people to slip away and flee for another six hundred or so miles through Montana. They finally surrendered after the battle of the Bear's Paw, near the Canadian border, about thirty miles from Havre. After the surrender, In Who Lise had escaped again and found refuge with the Pend d'Oreille Indians. But now, with Garcia's help, she wanted to locate and rebury her father's body and then find her way back to the ancient Nez Perce heartland in the Wallowa Mountains of Oregon.

Headed west again, she and Garcia encountered some of the same obstacles on the trail that Lewis and Clark had fought their way through. Forests of lodgepole pine so dense that a horse could not be ridden between the crowded, brittle trees, where nothing grew for grazing but pine needles and bear grass and buckbrush. Barricades of deadfall that slashed bloody furrows along the horses' shoulders and flanks and came perilously close to breaking their legs. Grizzly attacks, rock slides, and peak after endless peak along the almost impenetrable boundary between Montana and Idaho. "Coming to the top nothing entered my mind, except a bitter curse," Garcia wrote, years later. "Where to find a place to get down and back out of here . . ."

With their packhorses loaded with the buffalo robes they

hoped to trade for cattle and land to start a ranch in Idaho or in the Wallowa Mountains of Oregon, In Who Lise and Garcia survived the hazards of the Lolo Trail only to encounter a more implacable barrier on the Idaho side. They had almost reached the settlement at Lapwai, then as now the heart of the Nez Perce reservation, when they came to an Indian camp. Although Garcia spoke very little Nez Perce, he could sense that these people were unfriendly. As In Who Lise conversed with them at length, he could see that she was becoming angry and unhappy. She turned to Garcia. "I have no more home in the Wallowas."

One of my Idaho friends, a historian who married a great-granddaughter of one of Joseph's warriors, explained to me what an English-speaking Nez Perce finally explained to Garcia in 1878, that the so-called Nez Perce War between the United States and the nontreaty Nez Perce in 1877 had pitted relatives against relatives, Christian converts against traditionals, band against band, and caused a breach within the tribe that remains unforgotten to this day. The men and women Garcia and In Who Lise met on the trail were members of an upper Nez Perce band who wanted to live and let live with the whites, and they saw Joseph's band as renegades and murderers who had brought trouble upon the whole tribe. They warned In Who Lise that, if she continued on to Lapwai, the Indian agent was likely to arrest her as a member of Joseph's band and send her into exile in Oklahoma, and that Garcia, as the husband of a renegade, would never be allowed, by Indians or whites, to live in peace in Nez Perce country.

Gold fever had brought far worse troubles to the Nez Perce tribe than their own nontreaty warriors ever did. When prospectors trespassing on the reservation north of the Clearwater in the late fall of 1860 found traces of gold in a stream they named Orofino Creek, the inevitable stampede of gold seekers demanded access to Indian lands. As more gold was discovered, mining camps became settlements—Pierce, Elk City—and Indian trails became wagon roads. Federal troops were established at Fort Lapwai to protect the Indians from the prospectors—or was it the other way around? By 1863, the United States government was negotiating with the Nez Perce tribe to reduce their lands by 90 percent. It was their refusal to sign the 1863 treaty that made "nontreaty" Indians out of Joseph's band, and it was their rebellion at the government's appropriating their ancestral home in the Wallowas that would culminate in their long flight over the divide to Montana in 1877.

Meanwhile, at the confluence of the Snake and the Clearwater, the present city of Lewiston, Idaho, got started illegally on Indian holdings as a tent depot to supply the miners. By August 1863, stern-wheelers were carrying cargo from Portland up the Columbia and Snake rivers and unloading at Lewiston, where the axes and rifles and shovels and whiskey and flour and beans were reloaded on packmules to be humped and grunted east into the mountains, often as far as the Montana gold camps, three hundred miles from Lewiston on the other side of the divide.

In this busy picture, the Indians became inconsequential. Until young nontreaty hotheads rampaged along the Salmon River in 1877, killing whites and stealing horses and inflaming their own people into war and flight, the Nez Perce were bit players on the fringes of the gold settlements, fit for a little menial work, farming and mining, tending mule trains, and having whiskey sold to them. The local legends were changing in theme and personae. During the eight years I lived in Lewiston, I learned the Magruder story, for example, which is well known in the Clearwater country but hardly ever told beyond its boundaries. Lloyd Magruder was a merchant and packer who led his mule trains of mining supplies back and forth across the divide between Lewiston and Bannack, Montana, twenty days on his way and twenty days back on what was then known as the Lower Nez Perce trail and today is a Forest Service road locally known as Magruder Corridor.

Magruder had left a Maryland plantation at a young age and tried his luck at mining in the California gold fields. When the easy pickings ran out, he moved over to the Sierra Nevada, opened a store, lost everything in a fire, and moved back to California to start all over. At the news of the Orofino gold strikes, he came up to Idaho (why do I feel as if I've told this story before?) and invested in pack saddles and a string of mules. He thought that, after he'd made his wad, he might go into politics. Maybe he'd be Idaho's first territorial delegate to the United States Congress.

In fact, nothing was noteworthy about Magruder's fate, which was to be robbed and murdered on his way home from Bannack with his mules in October 1863. His would have been just another violent death on the divide, except that down in Lewiston, a plump and balding little hotel-keeper named Hill Beachey (I'm not making this up) had a bad dream. In the dream he had seen his friend Magruder leaning over a campfire to light his pipe, and, looming behind Magruder with his face illuminated in the flames, his murderer raising his ax and bringing it down on Magruder's skull.

Oh, go back to sleep, said his wife, and don't tell that dream to anybody else, because they'll laugh.

By late October, Magruder and his pack train hadn't shown up in Lewiston on schedule and his wife and friends were beginning to worry. When, late on a stormy night, a man came into the lobby of Beachey's hotel, the Luna House (yes, that is what it was called) to buy passage on the next morning's stage to Walla Walla, Beachey thought the stranger looked familiar. He puzzled over that face for a few hours, then went in search of a warrant to stop the stage. The stranger's face was that of the man Beachey had seen in his dream, splitting Lloyd Magruder's skull with an ax.

Based on that recognition, the little hotel-keeper determined that he would bring his friend's murderer to justice. He wasn't in time to stop the Walla Walla stage, but he got his warrant, had himself appointed a deputy sheriff, and set out on a thousand-mile pursuit that Ladd Hamilton, a former Lewiston newspaper editor, researched for his 1994 book, *This Bloody Deed*. Catching up with his villain and three accomplices in San Francisco, Beachey arrested them and escorted them, in chains, all the way back by steamship as far as Portland and then by relays of stern-wheelers to Lewiston to stand trial. Three of the gang (one swore his innocence and testified against the others) were hanged in March 1864.

Another human impulse that seems to assert itself into the Westward Movement, almost spontaneously at the meeting point between so-called savagery and civilization, is tourism. In August 1877, a young couple from the tiny western Montana community of Radersburg, George and Emma Cowan, decided to go camping with friends in the newly established Yellowstone Park. Mrs. Cowan's brother, Frank, went along, and so did her twelve-year-old sister.

Anyone who has bumped shoulders with the August hordes and throngs in today's Yellowstone Park will envy Mrs. Cowan's account of her party's idyllic few weeks up until Thursday, August 23, when they met their first other tourists. It was the party of General William Tecumseh Sherman, who had chosen that summer to "do the park." From one of Sherman's scouts, the Cowans learned for the first time that there had been a fight between United States troops and the Nez Perce at the Big Hole. The Nez Perce had gotten away, nobody knew where, and the troops were trying to find them. Surely they weren't fleeing through Yellowstone Park, surely the tourists were safe, but the Cowans noticed that General Sherman's party didn't linger, and they were just as glad that they themselves planned to start for home in the morning.

The next morning dawned. "I was already awake when the men began building the camp fire, and I heard the first gutteral tones of the two or three Indians who suddenly stood by the

fire," Emma Cowan wrote. Suddenly the woods seemed full of
Indians, who ate the Cowans' breakfast, helped themselves to
what was left of their flour and sugar, and, after the Cowans had
hastily packed their tents and camp gear, rode beside their wagons. Were the Cowans being escorted? Had they been taken
hostage? "Every Indian carried splendid guns, with belts full of
cartridges," Emma Cowan wrote. "As the morning sunshine
glinted on the polished surface of the gun barrels a regiment of
soldiers could not have looked more formidable."

Emma Cowan had just gotten over her first fright when the
warriors' mood changed for the worse. More riders dashed up,
plans seemed to be changed, then "Shots followed and Indian
yells, and all was confusion." Her husband fell from his horse,
blood spurting from a gunshot wound in his leg. Emma Cowan
and her little sister had tumbled off their horses and were bend-
ing over him when one of the Indians shot him in the head.

A warrior strapped Emma Cowan behind him on his horse.
No question now that she and her brother and sister were pris-
oners. They rode for the rest of that day, uphill through dense
timber, until at dusk they reached the main Nez Perce encampment and were taken to a silent and somber Indian they were
told was Chief Joseph.

Joseph would not speak, but motioned to Emma Cowan to
sit down on a blanket. She was offered food, which she could
not eat, from the meal the Indian women were preparing over
campfires. "A squaw sat down near me with a babe in her arms.
. . . Seeing that I was crying, the squaw seemed troubled and
said to my brother, 'Why cry?' He told her that my husband
had been killed that day. She replied, 'She heartsick.'"

Forking paths that never quite converge. One of the
teenaged girls in Joseph's camp that night was In Who Lise, suffering from a bullet wound in her arm and bleeding from her
mouth, where a trooper had bashed her with a rifle butt and
broken her tooth after he had shot her. In Who Lise's father lay
dead at the Big Hole, his body desecrated. Small children lay

dead at the Big Hole. Women had been shot at the Big Hole and their babies clubbed to death. No one in Joseph's camp in Yellowstone Park the night Emma Cowan wept at his feet would not have been heartsick for dead friends and relatives.

The next morning, Emma Cowan and her brother and sister were given bread and matches, some of their own bedding, and two worn-out Nez Perce ponies in exchange for their own horses. A warrior they knew only as Poker Joe pointed them toward Bozeman, Montana, and advised them to *ride all night, all day, no sleep.* Numb and hopeless, they set out, the two women riding the exhausted horses and their brother walking. In the late afternoon of that same day, they met a company of soldiers who had been sent out from Fort Ellis to look for the Nez Perce. The soldiers saw them safely as far as Mammoth Hot Springs, where they found a wagon ride to Bozeman. Emma Cowan had been home a week before she got word that her husband had been rescued, badly wounded, but still alive.

Sixteen years after the Cowans' misadventure in Yellowstone Park, the divide had become tame enough to make a hunting party for three young New Yorkers seem almost routine. In the fall of 1893, young Mr. Carlin, Mr. Himmelwright, and Mr. Pierce, with their handmade rifles and shotguns and revolvers, traveled out by railway to Spokane, Washington, where they paused to buy horses, dogs, and supplies and to pick up a hunting guide and a camp cook before they rail-freighted their outfit down to Kendrick, Idaho. They themselves followed comfortably by passenger train, arriving in Kendrick on September 17 in chill and threatening weather. The season was dangerously late for a horseback trip into the Bitterroots, but they were young and hardy, and this was to be the adventure of a lifetime. They had their hearts set on trophy elk, moose, and bear, especially a grizzly bear. Killing a grizzly bear would be wonderful.

Up the old Lolo Trail the young men rode, with their guns and their cameras and their sketchbooks and journals. They caught trout and shot grouse to supplement the excellent camp meals that their cook, George Colegate, prepared for them. They ignored the old settlers they met, who warned them that an early winter was setting in, and they also disregarded the growing uneasiness of their own hunting guide. They were all experienced woodsmen, and they resented being treated like greenhorns just because they were from New York. And indeed, all went well for several days. Their only worry, other than impending snow, was that George Colegate, their cook, wasn't feeling very well.

George Colegate insisted that he was just fine. He'd feel better tomorrow, he didn't want to go back to Kendrick, he didn't want to spoil anybody's fun. By this time the party had reached the warm springs near the summit of Lolo Pass, miles from any medical help. Of course the young men didn't want to cut their hunting trip of a lifetime short just because their cook was sick. But as the snow began to fall, Colegate got worse. Everybody speculated. Was it stomach cramps? Appendicitis? He couldn't keep up with the camp work, he couldn't cook, soon he couldn't walk. The young men and their hunting guide found themselves waiting on the cook instead of the other way around. Then, alarmingly, he began to *swell*. And to *stink*.

The truth was that George Colegate was suffering from uremia. For years he had been living with an enlarged prostate gland. He could empty his bladder only by means of a catheter, and for whatever reason or reasons, he had not brought his catheter on the hunting trip with him.

At this point, the story wavers on the brink of farce. When Ladd Hamilton told me he was writing his second book, *Snowbound*, about a man who went hunting in the Bitterroots and died because he forgot his catheter, I thought he was joking. Oh no, it's not a joke at all, said my north Idaho friends, it's a very well-known story. And indeed, the story recovers itself, becomes a morality drama of the three young men who, finding themselves trapped on the divide by an early winter, abandoning their horses in a heavy snowfall, tried carrying their anguished and grotesquely swollen cook through drifts and brush and boulders, tried building a raft and floating him down the Lochsa, tried to get him to walk on his own, and at last, in a desperate attempt to save their own lives, left him to die on the bank of the river while they staggered and crawled and starved and nearly froze to death until, on November 22, they were rescued by a search party of soldiers. Of course all their trophies, including their grizzly hide, had been lost. The next spring, George Colegate's friends retraced their trail, found what was left of the cook's body, and buried it in a grave that can be seen today from Highway 12. Young Mr. Carlin, Mr. Himmelwright, and Mr. Pierce would be scorned for years to come as the cowards who had broken every law of the frontier by leaving a comrade to die alone.

Melodrama, farce, morality, romance, tragedy. Perhaps the frontier can be redefined as the meeting point between conflicting narratives, and perhaps those narratives conflict within ourselves as often as with others. Did Emma Cowan, in her weariness and despair, really perceive in Chief Joseph's face an embodiment of the "noble red man," as she wrote years later, or did she look back through those years in the illumination of history and remember grace and dignity on a face that must have been as weary as her own? For the rest of her short life, was In Who Lise homesick? We know that she and Garcia left Nez Perce country and recrossed the divide to Montana, and that she was killed within the year in a skirmish with the Blackfeet, and that Garcia buried her in a rock slide near the Marias River, and that he remembered her in his old age when he wrote his memoirs.

Did Meriwether Lewis experience an inner disintegration as he traveled into the heart of an inexplicable landscape? What do we make of Hill Beachey's dream? And how do we assess the desperation and futility of the three young New York hunters as they tried to justify themselves against the force of the narrative as George Colegate's friends told it?

These stories provide no answers, and most are little known beyond the immediate region in which their actions occurred. They have not become part of a better-known western folklore, I think, because their truths—not their literal truth, but the truths they tell about place and the ways in which place affects our innermost selves—depend so completely upon the landscape of the divide. Barry Lopez believes that our minds are shaped by landscape as they are by our genes, and that stories are the threads that connect our intellect and spirit to the outward existence of rocks and hills and rivers. If, as Lopez says, interior landscape is a metaphorical representation of exterior landscape, we can understand Meriwether Lewis's terror when those threads were snapped.

Idaho was so stark, I remember thinking the first time I crossed the divide. I didn't think I would ever get my bearings. The shadows of Idaho were so sharp-edged, the proportions so gargantuan, the bluffs so barren. The species of sagebrush and weeds were subtly alien, the light didn't linger on the river or on the basalt cliffs the way I thought it should, and the clouds didn't bump me on the head as they had on the prairie. Even the storms blew in from the wrong direction.

My loss of balance can have been only a passing flicker compared with the shock of those who crossed the divide ahead of me. I live, after all, in an age of chain stores and sitcoms and the internet, classical music on Northwest Public Radio, and Prairie Oyster playing on Country KCLK out of Lewiston, Idaho. But here on the western side of the Bitterroots, where the bare river bluffs open out into the ancient floodplains and the deep plummeting drop of the Columbia River on its way to the Pacific, I am not the person I was on the prairies of the east front.

Still, I cross and recross the divide, where the rivers change direction and the stories strike sparks like stones. What is a divide, if not for crossing?

It has been twelve years since I first came to Idaho. Rachel's father is dead, and I live with her and Misty, my foster daughter, and three cats and a dog in the little university town of Moscow, Idaho, in the rolling hill country of the Palouse. I teach creative writing at the University of Idaho, and sometimes my students tell me, "You're from Montana, and Montana is glamorous. We're just from Idaho, and we don't have anything to write about!"

The shock of landscape may have led these students to believe that Idaho hasn't been invented, has no stories to tell, but after twelve years I have imagined my way here. I recognize the colors now, the deep blonde grass of summer, the basalt outcroppings as dark as shadows, the groves of blue-green pines on the hills above the wet brown furrows that tinge to green in spring and fall, ripen to gold, and fade into straw. And I watch for the hawks that own the telephone poles along Highway 95, which runs north and south through Idaho.

"What are you doing?" asks Rachel one autumn afternoon. We're on our way from Moscow to her piano lesson in Lewiston.

"Oh, just waving at that hawk I recognize. I think the hunting must be good from that particular crossbar, because that's where I always see him. Once or twice I've watched him dive into the stubble and come up with something alive in his talons, a mouse or a rabbit—"

I'd like to explain more. That a wave is my awkward acknowledgment, the only one I know how to make. That a hawk is a hawk and won't wave back.

Rachel rolls her eyes with a fifteen-year-old's sophistication. "Oh, that's great! That's just wonderful! I've got a mother who waves at hawks!"

Local Legend

. . . I was country
When country wasn't cool.
—BARBARA MANDRELL

STATE HIGHWAY 81, WHICH ANGLES NORTHWEST through Fergus County, in the dead center of Montana, is the main road between Lewistown, the county seat, and the tiny wheat-growing community of Denton. Most of the traffic on these thirty-odd miles is local. I used to cut across on Highway 81 quite often when I drove down from Havre to visit my parents in Lewistown. But now that I've moved to Idaho, I hardly ever drive that road, and if I want to conjure up a certain grassy point overlooking the Judith River, I have to imagine it.

Highway 81 has been paved since the early 1950s, but when I was a child and living on the ranch where my father and mother raised cattle and hay in the shelter of the South Moccasin Mountains, the highway was graveled, and it took twice as long to get to town as it does now. Traces of gravel still stick to the old ruts that turn off the highway and follow the rim of the benchland. In a mile or two, the ruts will drop down into the valley where Spring Creek flows into the Judith River. This is

Horses against a backdrop of the South Moccasin Mountains, 1942.

the place that my great-grandfather thought the most beautiful he had seen on his long trip out from Pennsylvania as a surveyor for the Great Northern Railway, and this is where he filed a homestead site in 1882.

Here in the middle of Montana, the summer days stretch forever, unhurried, toward an unimaginable twilight. On a July afternoon, the sun beats down on the miles of benchland, ripening the wheat and shimmering at the far edges. Every fence post seems to anchor a meadowlark in full throat, whistling those six fat notes that drift with the heat and the dust and the rich scent of sweet clover. Who can believe in the passing of time on a day like this? In a pasture across the highway, a diamond willow has sunk its roots into a dry creek bed for water. Cattle drowse in the crisscross shade of the narrow willow leaves, but they don't bother to turn an ear toward passing traffic.

Even in imagination, when I stop at the grassy point that overlooks the Judith River, I come up against the emptiness of the present. On this overgrown bank were three mailboxes on a plank mounted on posts, waiting for the occasional driver to pull over, crank down a window, and reach for his mail. One of the mailboxes was ours, one belonged to my great-uncle Theo

Hogeland, who ranched across the Judith River from us, and one belonged to our neighbors, the Huffines, who farmed on the bench.

None of these people live out here now, hardly any are still alive. In this empty space, where the posts have been pulled out of their holes and the holes fallen in, and where the slightest breeze lifts a scent like baking bread and honey from the ripening grassheads and sweet clover, I may be the only one who, even in imagination, feels a shiver, as though I've just realized an absence, like the inexplicable theft of some small object of value.

My shiver is a familiar that always roused itself whenever I came in sight of this grassy point. A shudder, one might call it, a sensation that began in the hair at the back of my neck, rippled down my throat and arms, and culminated in my breasts, where it clenched my nipples into erection. I first felt it in this exact spot on the grassy point, when there were still mailboxes on the plank, and my mother had shifted the black 1946 Ford sedan down into neutral and reached out the cranked-down window for the mail. The air smelled as sweet as it does in memory. I was six years old, and I savored the sensation, wondering what had caused it. After that, I waited for it whenever we stopped for the mail, and it always came. I can almost, but not quite, will it awake.

In my teens I read about the phenomenon of déjà vu, and I imagined past-life experiences that might account for my shiver. The explanation I liked best was that I was receiving sensations from my long-dead grandfather, who had been a cowboy during the first years of the twentieth century. He had ridden rep for the old Huffine cattle outfit over these very miles and made himself a local legend before his early death from a fall from a horse. *Loss* was the meaning of his story. I told myself that something of deep but forgotten significance had happened to him *at this exact place*, and somehow the currents of that old trauma, like sound waves rolling fifty years behind an explosion, were shuddering through the bones of a granddaughter he never knew.

In my mind's eye, I look down across the great gash in the benchlands where the Judith River, a thin blue thread, winds north through bottomlands of irrigated hayfields and scrub brush and scattered cottonwood groves until it eventually reaches its mouth at the Missouri River. On the far side of the gash, level with the grassy point but seven or eight miles away, more benchland stretches its fading checkerboard of pale yellow wheat and pale brown summer fallow toward the hazy blue. The silver glint to the left is the old grain elevator at Ware, the glint to the right is the grain elevator at Danvers. These were towns, once, on a railroad spur, with depots and post offices and general stores and saloons. Danvers even had a hotel. But the ranch families who still live out here will drive thirty miles to Lewistown now, or even a hundred miles to Billings, to do their shopping.

It seems to me, in spite of the lazy snap and crackle of grasshoppers in the warm weeds, that time has been cranked up. My life feels like a film that has been speeding through a projector, faster and faster, into a blur of days, years, shortcuts, and lapses. The older I get, the less a year seems like a year, the less a day seems as long as it should be. If I could grow backward, would time slow down? I play with the idea of running the film in reverse, gradually slower to my childhood of gravel roads. Slower still, to a time when my grandparents would drive a team and wagon down the slippery ruts from their ranch on the slope of the South Moccasins, ford the icy Judith, and crawl— eight miles, an hour's drive—up through the snowdrifts on the grade to Ware, where they could catch the train for another hour's ride into Lewistown to eat Christmas dinner with my great-grandparents.

This film would roll backward through the recent past and the depopulation of the prairies and the drought years of the 1930s. It would show the little claim shanties of the 1910 homestead boom disassembling themselves into piles of fresh lumber to be hauled backward to the railroads, which in turn would be rolling back their rails and vanishing. Now the cattle empires are shrinking, the grazing cattle spitting out grass and bunching themselves into herds to trudge backward to Texas. Now there is nothing but grass. The blue troopers' wounds have healed, they've faded back where they came from, and the starving and defeated Blackfeet are proud again and mounted on their painted ponies. There goes a Blackfeet raiding party, backward from Crow country on the other side of the mountains. Slower, slower, because the ponies have dissolved to the southwest, and the hunters are on foot, and they and their dogs are walking backward through the sagebrush for the past ten thousand years.

Farther back than the hunter-gatherers of the Besant or Old Woman culture, it's hard to imagine how slowly the film crawls in reverse. Twenty thousand years ago, the temperature drops. The camera finds the tips of the great ice sheets, follows their retreat and advance and retreat over two million years. Records the deposits of boulders left in their wake. Feels the temperature rise. The dawn horse and the woolly rhinoceros give way, after sixty to eighty million years, to the dinosaurs, which watch the mountains of central Montana un-forming as lava un-explodes back into volcanoes and fissures. Eighty to a hundred million years ago, the dinosaurs shrink back on the evolutionary chain, while ancient seas and lakes fall and and rise and fall and, for time beyond measure, cover all I know of Montana landscape with tropical water.

As a child, I believed that the names of landmarks were as permanent as the hills. After my great-grandfather had claimed his homestead on prime bottomland along Spring Creek, where it runs into the Judith River, his children in turn filed claims on the slopes above the creek and built cabins where they lived while they proved up on their land. Carrie's homestead cabin, Gobbie's homestead cabin, Bess's homestead cabin. By the time I was old enough to ask questions, the cabins were piles of rotting logs overgrown with pigweed and thistles. I couldn't locate

Mary's grandfather with oxen, about 1910.

them today. But if my grandmother were still alive, she would stand beside me on this grassy point and point out every site.

My grandmother taught me other names. The Grandma's Trees (giant cottonwoods in the middle of a hay meadow, left uncut because my great-grandmother Hogeland loved them), the Sheepshed Bottom (because my great-grandfather built his first sheep shed there), the Water Coulee (because it flash-flooded every spring.) And every cattle trail, every river ford had its story—that's the hole in the crick where the roan colt drowned—that's the pasture where the grass fire burned almost as far as the granary—and all the stories were ours, about a private landscape that had taken one family a hundred years to claim and put roots down into, to leave, and to die.

Behind me to the south, another private landmark juts out like a sentinel from the slopes of the South Moccasin Mountains. A butte with bleached ramparts of sandstone, capped with pines and striated from centuries of wind, left standing twenty million years ago when the last of the snowmelt from the ice age burst through its obstacles in a catastrophic flood that tore this river channel out of the high prairie. Probably it has had many names. Our family has always called it Theo's Butte, although it has been thirty years since my great-uncle owned the land and farmed around the base of the butte.

Theo's Butte has been the focus of local legends for years. In fourth grade I went to a one-room country school, southeast of here on the Denton highway, where the kids swapped stories about someone who knew someone who had collected a Mason jar full of Indian beads from up on the butte. *Finding treasure* was what we thought that story was about, like the other stories we had heard about lost caches of Indian artifacts. One story told about a man who had worked for Uncle Theo. He had explored one of those cracks in the cliffs and found beaded saddles and weapons and beautiful clothing, but by the time he came back with ropes and a shovel, a landslide had buried the treasure trove—*it's still buried up there, somewhere.*

These were not stories that adults willingly told, although occasionally somebody's dad would grudgingly admit to having known the one about the beads or the buried saddles and weapons. We children might have thought the stories were about buried treasure, but our parents knew they were about the shadowy people who had lived here before us, and the legends hung in the air we breathed, like a sickness our parents tried to protect us from. I was grown before I knew that everybody else knew that, in the 1870s, Crow Indians had camped in the cottonwoods at the mouth of the Little Judith River, about a mile below this grassy point, when they were stricken by an epidemic of smallpox. Indian parents carried their dead children up to the butte and left their bodies in the deep crevices in the sandstone. Twenty years later my great-grandmother, living in her homestead cabin below the butte, was afraid to let her children play on those cliffs because she thought that living smallpox germs might still be lying in wait in the dark places.

A prairie picnic, summer 1909. This photo was taken on a trip to look at homestead land. Left to right: Mrs. Camp and daughter; Mary E. Bennett Welch; Alfred P. Welch, holding daughter Sylva; small boy, a Camp child.

When I was ten, I was taken to a picnic on Theo's Butte. It was a family reunion, one of our last. I remember how our ranch trucks and the heavy cars of the California uncles lumbered over the ruts and boulders of the old wagon road that wound up behind the rimrocks, and I remember my surprise in discovering, when I jumped down from the bed of the truck to find my footing after the jolting ride, that the top of the butte, which looked so flat from a distance, was as rough and gullied as ordinary prairie.

The men lifted watermelons and cases of pop and beer out of the trucks. The women complained about the lack of water, but they started a dry camp and found a level place in the shade of jack pines to spread blankets and set out the ham and home-made rolls and chicken salad. When we cousins ran off to explore, they warned us, not about landslides or lingering small-pox germs, but about the rattlesnakes that denned down in the rimrocks and crawled out to sun themselves on the crumbling ledges of soft, gritty sand.

Landscape is perceived through a web of human spinning, and white settlers brought to the butte their own stories of violence. The butte holds at least one unmarked grave, a depressed oblong in the grass, hard to locate. Who is buried there depends on which story you listen to. It was a fight that broke out over a card game—no, it was a fight over water rights, and the man who was killed was buried on the spot. But the older women in my family tell a different story, about a stillborn baby handed to its young father. Penniless and bewildered, he wrapped the little body in a quilt and carried it up to the butte and buried it above the rimrocks before he rejoined his outfit and went overseas in 1942.

In 1882, my great-grandfather had written home that the Montana Territory was rich in resources of grass, water, and timber. With good winter feed and shelter for livestock, the empty territory was waiting to be transformed into ranchland by his hard work. As for the Indians who had hunted on the land he filed upon, he noted in one of his journals, "Away they drift, these conquerors of the coyote and wolf, alternately gorging and starving, against whom the white man has 'sinned' in killing off the buffalo thus removing their 'feast without effort.'"

He sent for his wife, who left the ten-room family home in the shade of hardwood trees and traveled west from Pennsylvania with a baby in her arms, by train and stagecoach, to join him in a cabin in the sagebrush. Whereas his stories had been about the West as an adventure, with himself as a protagonist pitted against weather and place, hers were about disasters averted by the narrowest of margins. Berrying with her children and stumbling into a den of rattlesnakes. Scaring a herd of cattle away from her cabin by firing at them with a ten-gauge shotgun that knocked her flat with its recoil. Giving directions to the Judith River to a man who drove up to her door with a team and a covered wagon. When it turned out that he was a murderer, hauling the bodies of his five victims down to a gravel bar where he buried them, she supposed it had been only luck that kept him from adding her and her children to the load in his wagon.

Stories give shape to that which has no shape, meaning to that which eludes meaning. How else could my great-grandfather justify his ownership of the land he lived on? How else could my great-grandmother voice the threat of an empty horizon? Or the terror of meaninglessness? By the time her children were old enough to listen, they could not hear what she was telling them. Instead, they idealized her. In an unpublished manuscript entitled "The Hogelands in Montana," one of her sons wrote,

> During this discourse little mention has been made of my Mother. While she had no direct part in the building of tunnels and ditches and houses and other similar jobs, you can believe she had a vital role in all the activities of her family. She was my father's guiding light as he was her shining knight. . . . I could write a book about our Mother, and her children. Instead, I will simply say that Mother's children adored her.

For years I have wondered what my great-grandmother's unwritten book might have contained. But except for the fragments, her narrative has been erased.

So how do I explain the shiver I feel in the dead center of Montana?

One autumn day in Alberquerque I listened to the Navajo poet Luci Tapahonso explain Diné mythology and its connection to landscape, and I understood dimly how the rocks and cliffs of the Southwest were underpinned by a system of story-telling that preceded creation and was understood and accepted by a whole people. (Yes, but untranslatable, another Navajo woman explained to me much later. She had been brought up traditionally, learning English as a second language, and she said that she could hear the sacred connections when she talked with her father in Navajo, but not in English.) I felt the impoverishment of my own tradition. In comparison with Navajo genesis stories, my family stories seem less organic than imposed upon the butte, arbitrary and tenuous and always private. And yet these stories are all I have.

My great-uncle Theo was a younger brother of that romantic long-dead cowboy, my grandfather. Theo was born on the homestead in 1889, the year Montana became a state. By the time I was old enough to remember him, he was a tough little man with bright blue eyes and a deeply tanned face. Nothing about Theo was glamorous. To the scorn of his brothers and nephews, he rode horseback in laced boots and a baseball cap, and he shortened his stirrups until his knees were flexed almost like a jockey's, but everybody admitted that he was as good a hand with a horse as anybody in the country. In his eighties he was still breaking colts to ride. Like all the Hogeland men, he was fond of children.

My father used to tell a story about Theo that took place before I was born. Underlying my father's story was the belief that, in a place where loss was a daily risk, an excess of emotion was a danger to everyone. Better to swallow the pain, deny the pain, and go on. Not even children were to be indulged. But it seems to me now that, to explain my shiver on the grassy point, Theo's is the story I would choose, because of course I have a choice of stories, and I have a choice in the way I tell it, which would not be my father's choice.

Theo's wife had died suddenly, leaving him with a ranch and four small children. The youngest child was a girl of three, my cousin Tobe. Tobe cried for her mother. She would not allow her aunts to console her, she clung to her father and refused to be separated from him. And so—what was he to do with a sobbing child hanging on his leg, when he had to finish his spring seeding—Theo took Tobe with him to the field on the slope below the sandstone butte. Holding her on his lap, he rode the iron seat of the drill for hour after hour, day after day behind his team of six horses as they plodded their rounds and the seed wheat spilled into the furrows.

*He seeded that whole hundred and sixty acres below the butte
that spring, drove six head of horses and worked the drills with that
kid on his lap*—but that's my father's voice, telling about a man
who spoiled his daughter.

Today, as I imagine the hazy taupe and gold of summer
wheatfields running all the way to the steadfast line of the butte
with its crown of jack pines against the rolling cumulus, the
shiver of meaning feels far different from the way I once interpreted it, through a teenager's romantic idea of déjà vu. I see the
six horses leaning into their collars. Their big hooves sink into
the ploughed soil as they plod. Sun burns on the tips of their
hames, their harness rings jingle, their big bodies creak and
gurgle with their effort. Behind them, larks spurt out of the
fencerows and dive for the harvest of worms. A hawk circles.

The man on the iron seat of the drill has his hands full of
lines and his head turned to watch his drilling pattern. Tonight
his neck will ache. The little girl on his lap has her thumb in her
mouth and her head on his shoulder. How she can nap through
this jounce and jolt, he doesn't know, but he cradles her as best
he can, as they ride in their cycle at the slow pace of horses in
this exact place, in a story about a grieving child and a father
who would not leave her to cry by herself.

Horses in Nightmares

STORIES ARE A WAY OF EXPLAINING THE INEXPLICABLE, of giving shape to that which has no shape, meaning to that which eludes meaning. Without stories, the first white painters who ventured into the West saw space without end, indescribable lights and shadows, unfamiliar beasts and men. In the oils and watercolors of Bodmer, Caitlin, Bierstadt, and Audubon, we can see how they wrestled with amorphousness. George Caitlin, trying to articulate his struggle with landscape in 1832, described the badlands of Montana as an "unsystematic and unintelligible mass of sublime ruins." Karl Bodmer, who had traveled along the Rhine River and painted its castles, took a steamboat up the Missouri River in 1833 and produced dozens of watercolors and sketches when he saw the White Cliffs. In his panorama *The White Castles on the Missouri*, he superimposed the ruins of the Rhine upon the White Cliffs, like castles in clouds, or perhaps like ghosts materializing out of a mist that seems to have caught the momentary attention of pronghorns watering in the river below.

Caitlin and Bodmer envisioned the West through a gauze of European culture. With their "sublime ruins" and "ghosts," they were bringing a nineteenth-century Romantic aesthetic to bear upon a landscape that otherwise eluded them. "The visitor's viewpoint, being simple, is easily explained," writes the cultural geographer Yi-fu Tuan. "The complex attitude of the native, on the other hand, can be expressed by him only with difficulty."

Between the simple and the complex lies an abyss. One of the first white women to try to explain her response to amorphousness was Nannie Alderson, who left a soft plantation life in West Virginia for her husband's cattle ranch in eastern Montana in 1883, the same year that my great-grandmother left Pennsylvania for central Montana. A half century later, Nannie reflected on her experience and wondered if she had gone crazy with isolation. "I was haunted by a demon of fear," she tried to explain to Helena Huntington Smith, who wrote down her story in *A Bride Goes West*. "I can't remember when it began to grow on me, but I know that until I lived on Muddy I had never been afraid except those few times I was left alone. . . . But now I was nervous about one thing or another all the time."

Nannie had brought with her a set of assumptions about Montana. She never expected to live there long; she thought that she and her husband would make a quick fortune raising cattle and go home to a life of luxury and leisure. While she supposed that, in unsettled territory, she would find freedom from trifling social restraints, she never seemed to realize the contradiction in her blithe confidence that the social structures of the agrarian South would follow her wherever she went and keep her safe. She believed that gentility mattered, that noblesse would oblige, and that her Northern Cheyenne neighbors would live up to her fantasy of the familiar and comforting role of the "darkies" she had known in West Virginia. But as the safety net of her assumptions dissolved, she was paralyzed by terrors that she was never able to articulate.

She knew, however, that her fear was focused on her husband's horses, and she knew it was not completely without a rational basis, because the stallions were so powerful and so violent that her husband carried a revolver when he rode near them.

Finally it did happen, this thing I dreaded. . . . On the same
impulse, as it seemed, the two great horses made a rush and each
one broke through his gate at the same instant as though it were
pasteboard. They met in the center, where they reared and
fought like bloodthirsty wild beasts or like the horses in nightmares, pawing and tearing at each other's throats. The men were
all there, with axes in their hands, but it seemed minutes before
they could stop them.

Eventually Nannie's worst nightmare was realized when her
husband was kicked to death by one of his horses, although,
ironically, by that time the Aldersons had left the ranch for the
relative safety of Miles City. Fifty years later, when Helena
Huntington Smith was portraying her as an intrepid pioneer
woman with unflinching eyes, how could Nannie explain why
she had refused ever again to live out of calling distance of children or neighbors?

A demon of fear, Nannie had called it. It was a fear of possession, which is another way of expressing the cackle in the
dark, the disintegration of flesh into the roar of chaos, the age-
old fear of personal annihilation.

Into those landscapes colored by European romanticism, Bodmer
and Caitlin painted strange animals. Supple, elongated beaver
and muskrat with human eyes. Enormous buffalo with tiny legs,
horned and glaring. Horses look almost carnivorous, with their
outstretched jaws and their daubs of paint for eyes, like the holes
in skulls. They race across the prairie on legs extended before
and behind in the curious way of nineteenth-century representations, as though they are suspended on invisible wings.
Caitlin's horses in particular seem to fly in swarms, undifferen-
tiated and feral. I don't know that I would even recognize them
as horses if I met them out of context.

This winter I dreamed of a three-eyed horse. It had been harnessed to a ruined wagon, and it watched me with two of its

eyes, like the two eyes on the same side of a Picasso woman's profile. Its third eye was on the other side of its head. Surely it was
blind in one of those eyes, I thought. Surely it was a mutant—a
monster. But then I saw that all three eyes rolled in their sockets
to follow me, and I realized that it was the horse itself that was
dead and stiff as lumber wrapped in a mummified hide.

Monster, from the Latin *monstrum*, means a prodigy or a por-
tent. Applied to humans, it is likely to imply monstrosity, as in
monstrum horrendum or *immanissimum ac foedissimum monstrum*. Applied to animals or events, it is likelier to imply the
wondrous or the marvelous. In classical literature, the monster
often is a sea creature and, through its association with the sea,
a source of life and power. At the same time, in Judaeo-Christian
tradition and in the earlier mythologies, sea monsters often
symbolize the exact opposite of life: death, hell, or the chaotic
powers of nature.

By definition, the monster must be singular, isolated, lonely.
Because it is the only one of its kind, its threat to the common
herd is the fascination of the mutant, the disturbed genetic code,
the unlicked cub carried in the rapist's seed. Perhaps its evidence
of the animal in the human is kept hidden, like the Minotaur at
the center of its labyrinth. Or perhaps it is a maternal monster,
like the Medusa, to be feared and hunted, its head of serpents to
be hacked off by the hero, for whom murder is a sublimation, a
denial of those impulses in himself that are indistinguishable
from the impulses of the monster he slays.

"Every man kills the thing he loves," wrote A. B. Guthrie, Jr.,
whose six major novels trace the history of white settlement in
Montana from the heyday of the beaver trade in *The Big Sky* to
the opening of the Oregon Trail and the development of the
great cattle empires in *The Way West* and *These Thousand Hills*,
and on through the homestead movement and the advent of the
Second World War in the *Arfive* novels. The Montana of *The
Big Sky* is an undefiled wilderness, an earthly paradise in the eyes

of the white mountain men who are drawn by its beauty and its promise of freedom from the restraints and corruption of civilization. It is a place where the natural grandeur of mountains, streams, and prairie is enjoyed by those savage children of innocence, the Blackfeet.

But the paradise is doomed, because the mountain men carry the seeds of its destruction with them. Every man of them, Guthrie emphasizes again and again, kills the thing he loves. Boone Caudill and his fellows wipe out the beaver, they infect the Indians with whiskey and syphilis, and they open a devastating trail into this rugged garden of Eden for white settlers and their families. By the third novel of the series, Lat Evans looks at the abused and eroded hills of Oregon and sees crowds of faces and a filthy river. What can Lat do but ride into the "thousand hills" of northern Montana in search of another new beginning? What can become of his youth and zest but loss and disillusionment, as he pays the price of existence? What can become of the landscape?

The first of the *Arfive* novels is set in the early years of the twentieth century in a town very like Choteau, Montana, where Guthrie himself grew up. By now the opportunities for a fresh start in an untouched paradise are running out. The last open prairie is about to be homesteaded, and an escape from civilization into wilderness will no longer be possible. The central character of *Arfive* is a schoolmaster who feels "a touch of discomfort, for he was part as well as agent of change." Even with his premonition, Professor Collingsworth doesn't realize the consequences for himself, but as surely as Boone Caudill, he, too, will kill what he loves—his wife, May, who dies from overwork and too many pregnancies. And in the sequel to *Arfive*, Collingsworth's daughter and son-in-law must deal with social, political, and environmental issues brought to crises by the irresponsibilities of the past.

From mountain man to schoolmaster, Guthrie lets nobody off the hook. His Montana story is a series of aggressions in the name of freedom and opportunity. Aggression against the land, aggression against the Blackfeet, aggression against women like Teal Eye and May Collingsworth, and aggression against the future, as Guthrie hammers down his lesson.

Like the sea with its vast space and unexplored depths, its associations with the source of life and the source of death, its divine connotations and its links with the old chthonic gods, the frontier carries the double symbolism of the divine and the demonic. But in Guthrie's apocalyptic vision, the victim becomes the monster and the aggressor becomes the threatened innocent. Mindless, perverse, the monster innocent speaks with the voice of a killer, *Get it before it gets you!*

How much of the language of the West is adversarial. Subdue it, dominate it, manage it, ride it with Spanish spurs and a spade bit, but break it to ride before it breaks you. The homestead reminiscences often put it bluntly. *We fought the weather. We fought the sod. We fought the snow and the mud and the roads. We fought the droughts and the grasshoppers.*

But fifty years after the publication of *The Big Sky*, we realize that the story is far more complex than we ever dreamed. Montana's first Native American novelist, D'Arcy McNickle (who, when he submitted his draft of *Wind from an Enemy Sky* to a New York publisher in 1936, was told that it wasn't "Indian" enough), inverted the fantasy of escape. The tribal past for McNickle's characters is a source of strength; for them, the terror lies in forgetting the past. Old Catherine in McNickle's *The Surrounded* lives long enough to discover that "in old age she looked upon a chaotic world—so many things dead, so many words for which she knew no meaning. . . . How was it that when one day was like another there should be, at the end of many days, a world of confusion and dread and emptiness?" Contemporary Native American writers have followed McNickle back to their center. Sylvester Yellow Calf in James Welch's *The Indian Lawyer* finds in landscape an acknowledgment of self that is almost transcendental in tone.

Many times when he was far away, Sylvester had envisioned these plains, the rolling hills, the ravines, the cutbanks and alkali lakes, the reservoirs and scrublands, and he always saw life. He saw a hawk circling over a prairie dog town. He saw antelope gliding through, over and under fences at a dead run. He saw a rattlesnake sleeping on a warm rock, or coiled, tongue flicking, tail rattling, as it slowly undulated back away. He saw beauty in these creatures and he had quit trying to explain why. It was enough to hold these plains in his memory and it was enough to come back to them.

The old narrative of doom required women's faces and Indians' faces to be crowded to the margins of the pages, their voices silenced with the sounds of rivers and the eloquent eyes of animals. Many of the contemporary women writing in the West seem to have realized that, if each man kills what he loves, they are among the targets. For some of these women, the terror of annihilation has become external, even global, threatening themselves and the animals alike. Ruth McLaughlin, who grew up in eastern Montana, concludes her short story "Seasons" with a ranch woman who imagines horses running from a thunderstorm. Unlike Nannie Alderson's horses in nightmares, Ruth McLaughlin's horses are as vulnerable as the ranch woman, who doesn't fear the horses but fears what they fear.

> She remembers when she had first come to Montana, it was just at the end of the war. The train had dropped her down from the mountains of the west coast onto the plains on the same day the bomb had fallen on Hiroshima. . . . That night, held in her new husband's arms, she had listened to her first thunderstorm in this new country; the sky crashed as though it would break and fall. She imagined the cows and horses in the pasture beginning to move at the first sounds of thunder, pressing into a herd, running now for shelter . . . but there was no place to run to. . . . She learned later that though they knew there was no shelter they raced anyway, tried to escape, pressed on together in the dark barely sensing in time where they might stumble; leaving behind them all the space that was dangerous, moving into some promise that was slightly ahead of them.

From being demons, horses can become *numen*, or intermediaries between human consciousness and landscape. Their power is double-edged. Like the horses in nightmares, they are likely to rouse from dreams or perhaps from art. Like tutelary spirits, they cross the divide between the simple and the complex, the known and the unknowable. In a poem called "Songs Were Horses I Rode," Ripley Schemm writes,

> *I know those stones asleep in my dream of prairie sky. Ice of a million*
> *Winds ago melted down their flanks, left them roaming wild*
> *Bunchgrass, some turned piebald with lichen, some scarred by storm.*
> *Let it be danger of rattler or rusted tine near your foot that wakes*
> *Them. Horses watch in their sleep. They rise and bolt for the ridge.*

My cousin Joe Murray is no longer young, and he is not quite my cousin. His mother was my grandfather's youngest sister. When he was a boy in his teens, he used to spend his summers on our ranch, helping with chores and learning what he could by following my father around. This was in the dirty thirties, when my mother and father were newly married and trying to scratch out a living between the ranch on the lower Judith and the pastures on the slopes of the South Moccasins that had been my grandfather's. It was still an age of horse-drawn agriculture, and my father got his plowing and seeding and haying done by breaking other people's draft horses to harness for a summer's use of them. Massive three- and four-year-old colts that had been crossbred from range stock with purebred Percheron or Belgian stallions would be driven, wild-eyed and snorting, into a corral where my father roped and hogtied them and "sacked them out" with a flapping saddle blanket until they were sweating and exhausted. A day or two tied to a snubbing post in the middle of the corral was long enough to call those colts halter-broken. Next they were harnessed to a wagon, with a contraption of ropes and straps, called a W, around their forelegs.

"Open the gate, Joe. Let 'em run."

With nothing in front of them but sagebrush and the two tracks of a dirt road, with the wagon rattling and bucking behind them, the colts flattened their ears and stampeded into thin blue air. Joe was holding the rope attached to the W that my father had told him to hold and trying to keep from being pitched out of the back of the wagon as dry grass and sandstone grit streamed past him.

It was a family joke from a time before I was born. "I looked around for Joe," my father would tell the story, "and there he was, picking himself up out of the dust."

"Hell, I was just a kid. I didn't know nothing," Joe told me years later. "Your dad yelled, *pull*, and I pulled on the rope and didn't wait to see what happened. I bailed out the back of that wagon and hit the ground rolling."

Pulling the rope had activated the W and jerked the colts' forelegs out from under them in mid-stride, dumping them into a thrashing pile of skinned legs and rasped breath. My father loved his horses, but he had been taught the old brutal, efficient ways, and two or three falls with a W was usually enough for any colt to start responding to a tug on the lines and a whoa.

Joe grew up to be a good hand with a horse, but times changed and the old harsh horse-breaking ways disappeared along with workhorse agriculture. In 1942 the Japanese attacked Pearl Harbor, and Joe dropped out of high school that winter and enlisted in the navy. My earliest memory of him is by kerosene light. I couldn't have been more than three years old. Joe had come out to the ranch to say good-bye, and he ate supper with us that night in the kitchen of the log house. He had brought with him the beautiful red-haired girl, Betty, whom he would marry, and I was spellbound and silenced in the presence of her and my tall cousin—nearly six and a half feet tall—in his navy dress blues that looked black by lamplight.

Times change. Joe came back from the war in the Pacific with an anchor tattooed on one forearm and a chain tattooed around the wrist of his other arm. He worked for my father for a while, but cattle prices were down, and eventually my father sold the ranch that had been his father's and grandfather's and bought another, more marginal ranch in the foothills of the Snowy Mountains. Joe found his bearings in the new world of mechanized agriculture, became a trouble-shooter for a farm implement dealer, and, on twenty-four-hour call during the long June and July days of haying season in central Montana, learned every graveled or gumbo road with an ailing hay baler at the end of it.

Meanwhile the world continued to change. The family was changing. It had been so large and close that, when I was very young, I believed that everyone I knew must be related to me in some way. But one by one, the circle of great-aunts and uncles was depleted. The children grew up, scattered, settled into their own families, their own lives. I finished high school, went off to the University of Montana, married and had children, ran off to graduate school and became the first divorcée in the family. And then my father died, taking with him all the stories, the lore, the old horse craft that had been handed down from generation to generation and that I didn't know I needed to know until it was too late.

But one summer day a few years ago, my sister Jackie and I drove through July heat and the smell of ripening hay to the grassy point overlooking the Judith River valley, where a row of mailboxes once had sat in a row on a plank mounted on posts. No mailboxes now, only Joe's dusty Suburban waiting in the weeds where he had promised to meet us and guide us around what he remembered of the old ranch. And there was Joe, big and ruddy as ever, though graying at the temples.

Joe drove us through the wheatfields on a narrow road I barely remembered. The only landmark I was certain of was the sandstone butte with its bristle of jack pine. And yet this had been the road we took to town, it had been the road to school, day after day—I felt as if I had wakened from a dream I couldn't quite remember.

Then the road fell over the edge of the river bluffs and snaked down through the shale and mica. In my childhood, this was the *hill*. You have to drive home down that *hill*, timid friends would exclaim, to the annoyance of my mother. Joe geared down and negotiated the rudimentary, eroded curves that hardly looked wide enough to accommodate the Suburban. Below us, the hill dropped straight down into sagebrush. I glanced at my sister, who had braced herself against the door. Memories were flooding back for me, of my father driving the old Ford pickup with chains on all four wheels, bucking through snowdrifts in January or skidding through gumbo mud in March, the grade so precipitous that it seemed certain we were about to slide over the edge—and nobody dared so much as squeal, not even my grandmother, because he had trained us all to be silent on the *hill*—but these weren't my sister's memories. She was only two when we left this place. She has been imprinted elsewhere.

Below us, the Judith River sparkled in its peaceful bend. Uncle Theo's barn still stood on its far bank, which seemed much closer now that the cottonwoods were gone, gone from the river and gone from what had been a hay meadow. A hunting consortium owns this property now, and apparently nobody bothers to farm or graze it.

The road circled the old meadow and climbed a low rise where I once played in the chokecherry groves that sheltered our house and barns and corrals, our lane and fenced garden. I kept thinking that there wasn't space enough here for what I remembered. Where had the house been, where had the log shed been? And my willow tree, with a board seat nailed into the high limbs? All gone now, even the chokecherries and willows bull-dozed out by a sometime owner who had tried to straighten out the loops and whorls of the creek and plant wheat. The creek had risen over its new banks and flooded him out, and only a gravelly residue remained of his efforts, or ours.

"There's the utility pole," Joe pointed out, "so the house must have been there."

I couldn't imagine it, couldn't bring it back.

We got back in the Suburban. Joe drove another half mile through the dreamscape, then through a wire gate and up a washed-out track that climbed between clumps of greasewood to the slopes of the South Moccasin Mountains where my grandparents had homesteaded. We had lumbered up that track every spring of my childhood for the annual cattle branding, because the corrals on the upper slopes dried out faster than ours did, and now I kept thinking that there should be white hawthorne in blossom, a scent of snow, and calves bawling. But of course a branding would have been weeks earlier.

And of course my grandparents' log house was long gone from the slope. Even its sandstone fireplace and massive chimney, which had stood pointing at the sky for years after the house was torn down, had fallen into the cellar hole and been bulldozed over. Nothing, nothing. Nothing to see except sky and the blue-green shoulders of the mountains crouched over the grass and sage in its lap.

Cutbanks sliced the slopes, and Joe knew the sheltered draw where, sixty years ago, he had ridden to wrangle the horses and found them mysteriously, staggeringly, sick.

"I'd saddled old Lucy after breakfast," he told us, "and rode out here, and when I found the workhorse bunch, I couldn't figure out what was the matter with them. They were silly, dizzy, like they could hardly walk, and when they did walk, it wasn't in a straight line. Poor old Pet, I thought I'd never get her up that trail to the barn, she was so weak and wobbly. And that was the first we'd seen of the sleeping sickness."

Equine encephalitis, they'd said it was. That year had been a ranch disaster with the horses too sick to do the spring seeding. I remember my father telling about it, and how he'd asked his uncle's advice about spending money on the new vaccine for sleeping sickness. *Kidder,* his uncle had told him, *it's a lot of money, but for anybody who cares about his horses the way you do, and can't bear to see them sick, it's the only thing to do.*

"Did most of the horses die?" I asked Joe.

"N-no. I don't think any of them died. They were sick for a long time, but they came out of it. They were never the same. Pet had seizures for years after that. She's the mare that threw you off and broke your arm when you were seven."

All the long-dead horses, all the forgotten names.

And nothing else to see up here, except the buffalo grass and clouds blowing past the mountains. Then I turned and saw, cutting through sagebrush and across the coulees in a line as exact and straight as a ruler, the remains of a fence. Tough cedar posts, aligned as perfectly as if by a surveyor and set to last a hundred years. A few strands of ancient barbed wire sagged off its staples.

"It's the old line fence," said Joe. And I realized that it marked the boundary line between my great-grandfather's homestead and my grandfather's.

"Who built it, do you think?" I asked.

Joe ruminated for a moment, then shook his head and laughed softly as he understood the question behind my question. "Albert, probably," he said.

We stood together in the ripe grass, each thinking our own thoughts. Albert was my grandfather, dead from a fall from a horse before I ever was born. My father had had only the faintest memories of him. And now here were these cedar posts, set by his hands in their arrow-straight march across prairie and coulee toward the butte. Although I knew that he had been brought up as I was not to speak of deep feelings, I also knew that associations were flooding Joe as they were me. He and I were perhaps the last persons left alive to sense the significance in that fence. Even my sister could feel only the silence. For the fence held no meaning in itself. It was a superimposition, a ghost of order. The cedar posts, desiccated by the years of wind and snow and sun, were more tenuous than the thin soil and the sparse grass.

For comfort, I thought of wild rides on nightmares. Of horses running from thunder toward the promise that lies slightly ahead. Of the horses Joe Murray remembered, and of boulders like sleeping horses. Of the double-edged power in horses, and the contradictions, and of all the ways that we try to deny the monster within ourselves. Let the wind erode, the rain wash away the soil, let our fragile boundaries decay. Let the stories remain.

Fort Assinniboine

A FEW YEARS AGO, WHEN THE MONTANA HIGHWAY
Department published a list of the state's worst highways in connection with an appeal for funding, they left
off State Highway 230, which branches off Highway 191 a few
miles north of Lewistown, winds around several mountains,
crosses the Judith River, and climbs northwest for ninety miles
through dry coulees and wheatfields and abandoned towns like
Coffee Creek, Square Butte, and Geraldine before it breaks out
of the sagebrush at Fort Benton on Highway 87. Highway 230
is one of the worst highways in Montana. But then, nobody
drives it but me.

I know this is true because I have never met anyone on 230.
I have seen other vehicles, occasionally. Trucks in fields, parked
as though forever, not just waiting for the next round of the
combine to gush out a load of wheat. Cars parked by empty
ranch buildings, buried in sagebrush. Wrecks, or in working
condition? Too far away to tell. As I daydream through the
white light and the dust and the illusion of water shimming
across the blacktop a mile ahead, I feel less likely of passing
another car than of catching sight of the old Métis, Bill Rivers,
slashing furiously at his team and careening across the cutbanks

in his screeching Red River cart, as he does in Wayne Ude's novel, *Becoming Coyote.*

Temperature extremes from minus forty in January to plus a hundred and ten in July are hard on a paved road, but Highway 230 really doesn't look much worse than it did three years ago, only a little rougher in the shadows of the cuts where the frost has sunk into the blacktop in winter and heaved it up in the spring thaw. In the distance, horses graze around the patches of saline seep that whiten their pastures, or they drowse in fence corners, stamping at flies, head to tail, in the shade of box elder trees that grow along the deep gluteal cracks of dry creek beds. The air is transparent. I dream about highways. Confluence, romance, the literary clutter a lifelong teacher can't sweep out. The highwayman comes riding, riding, riding through the night. English pilgrims ride on the king's highway through the dust and meadows and April shade to Canterbury. Roman highways aim straight through Britain for Scotland and the Picts. But out here on the depopulated high plains, the *highway* snakes down improbable grades and around curves for reasons that may be apparent locally but are lost on the transient driver at seventy miles an hour through the hundred-degree August heat and the smell of melting asphalt and sweet clover. Like the empty gray frame shacks that sag more drunkenly every year around the one remaining live bar in Square Butte, Highway 230 is warping and disintegrating into stretches of gravel that seem more profound every year, as though its lack of maintenance reflects a corresponding lack of will.

The Roman settlement of Britain lasted three hundred years and now is reduced to a scattering of place names, a ghostwalk or two, a note on the English lit syllabus, and a few eroded stones and implements in Bath or in the Museum of London. Human settlement in north-central Montana goes back ten thousand years, but recorded white exploration of the territory begins with the Lewis and Clark expedition in 1805, picks up momentum with the discovery of gold in the 1860s, and settles into farming after the Enlarged Homestead Act of 1909. The shacks I see from the highway, poking out of the sagebrush in shimmers of heat or stranded like derelicts in the midst of vast sculptured stretches of stubble, probably date from the homestead rush of 1910–1914. The homesteaders who survived the drought of 1919 have died, and their sons have retired or succumbed to the high interest rates of the 1980s or to the more recent drought. The young have moved to town or out of state to find jobs, and a handful of farmers cultivate their federally subsidized wheat with giant implements on thousands of these dryland acres. Eighty years, and farm culture on the prairie is crumbling at the edges.

But then, nobody has ever really owned the prairie. Ten thousand years ago those hunter-gathers, drifting across the Bering Strait and groping their way down the spine of the northern continent, paused here on the plains only a few thousand years, long enough to lose a handful of flaked tools, before they continued on down the isthmus and into the southern continent. Others drifted after them, drifted on. When white expansion drove Indian tribes out of their territories to the east, they carved themselves a place on the northern plains for a few hundred years until, in their turn, they were driven out by more powerful latecomers. Of the tribes we think of as indigenous— Blackfeet, Assiniboine, Cree—none can lay an earlier claim to north-central Montana than the seventeenth century.

Then we came, the last of the westering whites. What did we hope to find out here in these thousands of square miles of prairie between the mountain ranges of central Montana and the Milk River to the north?

And why, in 1879, did we feel the need to construct, on the brow of this bare empty stretch, just thirty miles south of the Canadian border, near present-day Havre, one of the largest and last military posts in the West?

Three years ago, Highway 230 was a regular shortcut of mine through Montana, a breakneck to meet deadlines. But this afternoon I'm taking my time, driving to Havre to see friends and to walk around the ruins of Fort Assinniboine, which a local committee is trying to get (and eventually will succeed in getting) on the National Register of Historic Places.

Looking for information on the fort, I had found Nicholas P. Hardeman's 1979 article, "Brick Stronghold of the Border," in *Montana The Magazine of Western History*, and learned that Fort Assinniboine was named for the Assiniboine Indian tribe, with the extra "n" inserted by the War Department for reasons best known to itself. The fort was established on a military reserve of one hundred thousand acres near the mouth of Beaver Creek on the Milk River. Its 104 brick buildings were mostly erected during a frantic anthillish five months of brick-making and construction. Astonished local Indians said that the fort rose out of the ground. Its initial cost, in 1879, was $100,000. By the time it was completed, in 1883, its cost had ballooned to $500,000. In 1894 it was regimental headquarters for the legendary Buffalo Soldiers of the Tenth Cavalry, but by 1903 it was little more than a guard post. In 1911 it was abandoned by signature of President William H. Taft.

At its peak, Fort Assinniboine was a self-contained bubble on the rim of the world, a realized fantasy, a space colony on the western plains, an ark on a shortgrass sea. Hardeman provides a list: cottages for the 36 commissioned officers and their families, barracks for 453 noncommissioned officers and enlisted men, quarters for Indian scouts; a guardhouse, a hospital, sutler's store, quartermaster and commissary warehouses, stables for 300 horses and mules; band quarters, bakery, sawmill, Signal Corps weather station, chapel, school; shops for blacksmithing, wagon wheel making, and saddlery; a granary large enough to hold a million bushels of feed grain for the livestock, a 52,252-cubic-foot-capacity root cellar, ice houses, and a 100,000-gallon water tower. All this construction took place more than seventy miles

by foot or horseback or freight wagon from the nearest connection with settlement and supplies, brought in by steamboat, at
Fort Benton. The echo of that self-perpetuating bustle sounds
like the activity on an institutionalized castaway's island, the
result, perhaps, of splicing Robinson Crusoe's genes with an ant
colony's.

In early newspaper accounts of the fort, I find some of the
fascination of reading about Crusoe's ingenuity. For instance,
the soldiers who planted gardens around the fort and posed with
their cabbages to have their pictures taken. Or the lieutenant
who invested in a pair of hogs and wrote home to boast that he
fed them on mess scraps and got his troop out of debt with his
profits. Castaways are what those first troops must have felt like.
How far is seventy miles on foot?

How far is seventy miles on foot if you grew up in New
York City, enlisted in the army, and were shipped first to
Georgia for basic training and then by rail and steamboat up to
the Montana Territory? If you disembarked at the Coal Banks
Landing into endless unsheltered wavering grassland and were
told that you were going to defend the northern border against
the Indians who killed General Custer? Would the seventy miles
seem longer because you were black and your officers were
white? You would have marched into the gray monotone of late
summer grass, through the shadows of clouds, toward the outline of the Bear's Paw mountains. A single blue butte loomed on
the horizon.

Holed up on the butte and shooting down on the recruits
were Indians that someone had erroneously told them were the
Crow. "But the Soldiers drove them off without the Indians
inflicting any damage to them," wrote one of those young men.
"They did not know what damage they did to the Indians as
they were on a big rock. That was the Soldiers last days travel to
where they would build the Fort. And as that was their first
meeting with any Indians since they arrived there, they expected
that there would be many more meetings of the same kind."

Camped for their first night on the unbroken sod of the future fort, in sight of the butte from which the Indians had fired on them, the walls of their tents must have seemed thin and the shadows unreliable to the young sentries. They could not have known that their tour of duty at Fort Assinniboine would be summed up in a word: dull.

For me, the seventy miles they covered on foot over several days is little more than an hour's drive. This afternoon I leave Highway 230 and cross the Missouri River at Fort Benton, turn north on the scarcely better maintained Highway 87, and cross the Marias River at Loma. A green respite of cottonwoods, then the long climb through the high plains toward the profile of the Bear's Paw and the butte where the soldiers came under fire in the late summer of 1879.

As I approach Havre, the remains of Fort Assinniboine are visible from Highway 87: a line of low gray hills, a distant cluster of three or four brick houses in the shade of cottonwoods, a few outbuildings, and, closer to the highway, three or four long mounds that are said to have been bulwarks for rifle practice. A sign identifies the site as an Agricultural Experiment Station of the Montana State University and warns against trespassing.

When I first came to live in Havre, the old fort was *out there*, but uncompelling. Every new faculty member was told that bricks from Fort Assinniboine had been salvaged to build Northern Montana College's Pershing Hall, a crumbling vault named after the fort's most famous soldier. Some said that it was a pity that Fort Assinniboine had been allowed to disintegrate. The Canadians, after all, had struck an economic gold mine on their side of the border by making a tourists' attraction out of Fort Mcleod, and at one time we might have done the same with Fort Assinniboine. But everyone agreed that we were too late. Too much had been razed or scavenged. Too little remained to hint at a time when, band playing, children chasing, guard-house overflowing, rifles crackling at targets, men blacksmithing, wheelwrighting, saddlemaking, and trading in the back lot with supppliers out of freight wagons and Red River carts, those 104 brick buildings had seemed as permanent as the sod they had risen from.

Still, taking the Frontier airlink flight from Havre to Billings one June evening, I glanced out the window and caught my breath as the plane left the airport pattern and banked over the prairie south of town on its way toward the mountains. I did not realize what I was seeing, at first, laid out below me like an indelible map, squares and rectangles as true as they had been drawn in 1879, parade grounds and foundations and perimeters, miniaturized by altitude but embedded as deeply as ever in the brow of the country. As I recognized the grid of Fort Assinniboine, it was gone. The plane leveled out of its bank and climbed to cross the Bear's Paw on its way south, and the lines of the fort fell away. But I will never forget that glimpse of the past upon which the present had been superimposed. Certain of our actions remain with us for good.

In 1876, in the aftermath of the Battle of the Little Big Horn, Sitting Bull fled to Canada with his surviving Sioux and camped in the Cypress Hills, fifty miles north of the Montana border. In 1877, after Chief Joseph's surrender to General Miles following the Battle of the Bear's Paw, some of the nontreaty Nez Perce escaped to Canada and sought refuge with the Sioux. It is perhaps more apparent now than it was in 1877 that these two battles marked the climax of thirty years of war by the United States upon the Plains Indians, although the Indians would try to defend their land for another thirty or so years. But in 1877, public uproar at the death of General Custer and the "Sioux threat" was enough to justify the initial funding for Fort Assinniboine.

But while the literature published by the Fort Assinniboine Preservation Association explains that the fort was constructed to protect white settlers from the Indians, neither the Sioux nor the Nez Perce survivors seemed a serious enough threat even to contemporaries to account for a military installation on such an enormous scale. For one thing, there were no settlers (legal settlers, at least) to protect. In 1879 the Montana Highline was still part of the giant Blackfeet Indian Reserve, which stretched from the Dakota border to the Rockies. The settlers who were outraged by Indian depredations were over a hundred miles to the south, along the Sun River, and the military protection they clamored for was not against the fugitive Sioux or Nez Perce but against the starving Canadian Cree, who frequently slipped across the border to hunt the ever-scarcer buffalo but who could hardly have provided exercise for a northern garrison of nearly five hundred troops.

A more startling theory to account for the vast size of the fort was current in the Montana Territory at the time its construction began. Senator James G. Blaine of Maine dreamed of becoming president of the United States and acquiring an empire. "A desire on the part of the army to help Mr. Blaine annex Canada . . . may have had something to do with the establishment of this post," speculated the *Fort Benton River Press* in 1889.

To Montanans who have lived for years along the most easygoing international boundary in the world, where farms sprawl across both sides of the border and Canadian coins rattle almost as frequently as American change, the idea of annexing Canada seems a little less lunatic in the shadow of Fort Assinniboine and all its grim masonry. And yet, and yet. A more prosaic reason why those walls of claustrophobic brick rose out of the earth is that somebody was making money out of them.

The man who garnered Fort Assinniboine's first construction and sutler contracts was the pioneer territorial entrepreneur Charles A. Broadwater, who saw his opportunity from the start. Correctly gauging the pressures that soon would open the Blackfeet Reserve for white settlement, already negotiating with American financier and railway promoter James J. Hill to build his railroad across northern Montana, Broadwater held the strings of personal and political influence and knew how to pull them into a design of his own.

Broadwater was a Missourian who had followed the gold rush into Montana but quickly discovered a more dependable profit in hauling supplies to the mining camps than in chasing gold himself. Apparently he had a talent for making friends. The historian William Lang has described him as able, astute, and highly likable. His friendship with Major Martin Maginnis, the Montana Territorial delegate whose lobbying in Congress helped to earmark that initial $100,000 for the construction of Fort Assinniboine, probably also helped Broadwater to secure his contracts to supply timber and make bricks for the new installation. In fact it was Broadwater who, with a labor force of soldiers, 500 Métis, and 350 civilian laborers, and with a brick-making machine that turned out 25,000 bricks a day, caused the fort to rise out of the earth. "In five months the work was practically finished at a cost of $500,000," noted the *Helena Weekly Independent* in 1889. "It may be incidentally remarked that Col. Broadwater's business sagacity was rewarded with a good part of this sum, and in addition he secured a post trading sinecure."

A photograph I had always thought was of officers' quarters turns out, according to Lang's profile of Broadwater in *Montana the Magazine of Western History*, to be of the entrepreneur and his family on the porch of their brick house at the fort.

The house in the photograph is ample, but it has the heavy, constricted look of the fort's barracks and warehouses. Unfenced, it sits four-square on a flat patch of prairie that ends only with the limits of the camera lens. With its narrow windows, its over-hang, its intrusive bulk in otherwise uninterrupted space, the house is an agoraphobe's dream.

In the foreground, a trail has been trampled through the shortgrass. Studying it, I can almost feel the dry heat and the constant wind, but Broadwater seems not to notice. He sits casually on his porch steps with his legs crossed. He is that rare figure in a photograph, a completely unselfconscious subject. The achievement of the 104 brick buildings in five months' time seems hardly to have stirred him.

Two women sit in rocking chairs farther back in the protection of the porch. Their faces are indistinguishable. On the prairie sod beside the house, in its narrow shade, stands a third woman. She wears a long-sleeved, high-necked dress. She bends over a child in a perambulator; next to her sits another child on a high-wheeled tricycle.

Her dress sweeps the sod. I can almost see the fine dust accumulating on the dark fabric, the bleached grass seeds hooking their way into her hem. She is not necessarily anonymous. A little research might uncover her name and the names of the children she is caring for. But I am less intrigued by the shreds of her identify than I am in imagining her feelings. Does she sleep in a bedroom on the southeast corner of the house, as I did when I lived in Havre? At night does she lie awake and listen to the wind whine around those heavy brick walls? Does she feel the isolation so intensely that she wants to run, although she knows she has nowhere to run except out of the suffocation of her own flesh and bones? Does she think she will live in this space colony on the prairie long enough to see the bricks dissolve, to feel herself merge with air and dust? Or does she believe that her castaway's stay here will be brief, that the fierce light and space and weather will turn into dreams?

The bastions between her inward and outward space already are slipping, whether she knows or cares. On the porch steps behind her, the man dreams of cause and effect. Soon, with Broadwater's orchestration, James J. Hill will build a railroad across northern Montana. The whiskey community of Bullhook Bottoms to the north of Fort Assinniboine will be transformed into the town of Havre. The Blackfeet, of course, will have to go. Confined to a much smaller reservation to the west, they will face death by starvation, exposure, and disease.

Meanwhile, because a railroad needs commerce, Hill will

write and speak and lobby tirelessly for white settlement. Rain, he will assure the scores of bank clerks and teachers and tailors and concert pianists and doctors and dockhands and immigrants, follows the plow. Hill will promise prosperity on a hundred and sixty dryland acres. The Enlarged Homestead Act will become law and, for a few years, thousands of women in skirts that sweep the sod will live in the fragile shelter of homestead shacks dotting the prairie where young lieutenants from Fort Assinniboine now hunt wolves with hounds. Helping to bring all this change about, Broadwater will be hailed as Montana's favorite son.

Foreseeing the future, wearing his abilities easily, Broadwater can afford to relax on his heavily bastioned front porch in 1880. The one piece of information he does not possess is that he will not live to see either the realization of the dream of settlement or its crash. He will die suddenly in Helena in 1892, mourned by the men and women of Montana as one of the state's greatest promoters.

Whether Fort Assinniboine was born out of anti-Indian hysteria, or from Senator Blaine's dream of a North American empire, or from Charlie Broadwater's more modest dream of a business and political empire in the Montana Territory, the main occupation of its troops during its first sixteen years, other than raising cabbages and hogs, was chasing the Cree.

On October 19, 1881, a Lieutenant Doane wrote, "Day before yesterday we went out and jumped up thirty-five lodges of Crees at the lakes near Woody Island Creek. They packed up and went north without difficulty. . . . Found a camp at Woody Island Creek—about 138 lodges of Crees and half breeds. These we go after tomorrow." Months later, nothing had changed for Lieutenant Doane but the weather: "Burnt 100 shacks yesterday—only twelve men with me. Cold as Greenland."

Even in the context of the history of the Plains Indians, it is difficult to think of an unluckier people than the Cree. Drifting

west into the northern plains in the wake of the ever-scarcer buffalo, trying to keep themselves fed, the Cree seem to have possessed a curious, grim talent for being in the wrong place at the
wrong time. During the nineteenth century, they had hunted on
both sides of the border between Montana and Canada, but
when many bands signed treaties with the Canadian government in return for rations, one group of the Cree under Little
Bear refused to give over their traditional hunting lifestyle.
Instead, they retreated into Montana, and the resulting confusion about their national origins contributed to their grief.

In the aftermath of the 1885 Métis rebellion, which brought
the wrath of Canada and the United States down on the Métis
as well as their Cree allies, Little Bear's band of Cree became, literally, Indians without a country. Because they had refused to
sign their treaty, Canada regarded them as aliens, while Montana
argued that they were Canadian Indians. Impoverished, suspect,
hated by reservation Indians as well as by whites on both sides
of the border, two hundred Cree in Montana were reduced, during the hard winter of 1887—1888, to subsisting on the frozen
carcasses of several hundred coyotes that had been poisoned by
cowboys and thrown into a ravine.

Bitter complaints boiled out of the territorial newspapers.
Look at the dirty, thieving Cree! They'll eat garbage, they'll eat
poisoned coyotes, they'll eat carrion. They're hunting game out
of season, they're stealing cattle, they are disease-ridden beggars,
and they belong in Canada. The *Fort Benton River Press*, always a
mouthpiece for the most reactionary views of the frontier, wrote
that "the day has about passed when these lazy, dirty, lousy,
breech-clothed, thieving savages can intrude upon the isolated
households and nose around in the backyards of private resi-
dences in communities of civilized beings with impunity."

So out rode the soldiers from Fort Assinniboine with can-
nons and Gatling guns to locate the Cree, burn their lodges, and
chase them back to Canada. It was an exercise in futility. The
moment the soldiers headed back to the fort, numb from riding

in the minus-forty-five-degree cold of February or parched from the plus-one-hundred-degree heat of July, back across the border sneaked the Cree. It was sneak back or starve, because they could find no game on the Canadian side and, as nontreaty Indians, were entitled to no rations from Canada. For their part, the soldiers complained about the weather and the mosquitoes and the incomprehensible government policies that kept them from crossing the border and cleaning up the Cree once and for all.

So for sixteen years, while Broadwater ran his trading operation out of the back lot of the fort where the Métis traders lined up their wooden-wheeled Red River carts beside the giant freight wagons from Helena and Fort Benton, while Hill began his railroad and Montana moved toward statehood, the troops chased the Cree. Donations from sympathetic whites and desperate appeals for federal funds got the Cree through one or two of the worst winters. In 1892, James G. Blaine, who once had dreamed of empire and now was U.S. secretary of state, tried to deport the Cree permanently. The Canadians had finally agreed not only to accept them but to grant amnesty to Little Bear and others who had been implicated in the 1885 rebellion. Lieutenant John J. Pershing was sent out with troops from Fort Assinniboine to round up the Cree for the last time.

Pershing spent June and July 1896 combing the brush and coulees of a thousand square miles. He drove the Cree out of camps near Great Falls, Havre, Malta, Glasgow, Missoula, and Butte, and off several reservations. He also rounded up a number of Métis and Montana reservation Indians who tried to explain to the soldiers that they had made a mistake, but who were herded into Great Falls along with the Cree and loaded into boxcars for Coutts Station on the Canadian border.

The Cree on the Canadian reservations were starving. More frightening for the Montana Cree than starvation was the Canadian government's breaking the terms of their amnesty as soon as they had crossed the border. Little Bear and one of his followers were arrested for the murder of several priests during the 1885 rebellion. They were soon released for lack of witnesses, but their band had had enough. In spite of troops and Gatling guns, of being burned out of their shacks in subzero weather, of eating poisoned coyote carcasses, of being the target of newspaper editorials and the petitions of Christian clergymen who feared that Cree barbarism would hurt the territory's reputation, the Cree were back in Montana before the end of 1896. Pershing probably prayed for an early reassignment to Cuba.

Powerless, without resources, and nearly friendless, the Cree preferred starvation in Montana to starvation elsewhere. They may have lived there only for a century or so, they may have lacked any legal claim to it, but the shortgrass prairie of northern Montana had claimed the Cree, and they returned again and again to its winters and wind and light. Eventually their endurance repaid them a small measure. The greatest irony in the story of Fort Assinniboine is how, in the face of opposition from the *Fort Benton River Press*, the *Havre Plain Dealer*, the citizens of northern Montana, and the commissioners of Hill County, who traveled to Washington to protest against it, years after other tribes had been settled on reservations, on February 11, 1916, a bill was signed creating the Rocky Boy Reservation on a mountainous portion of the Fort Assinniboine military reserve for the landless Cree and the Chippewa. Seventy years later their children and grandchildren still subsist on the slenderest of means. Unemployment on the Rocky Boy Reservation is said to exceed 90 percent.

Now I walk through the ripe grass of August with the friend who for several years has been promising me a tour of the ruins of Fort Assinniboine. Montana finally got rain this summer, after several drought years, and the outlines of the parade grounds and the old foundations are hidden under a thick new growth of wild grass and buckbrush. While my friend beats the grass ahead of us with a stick for rattlesnakes, he tells me about the public tours he has been conducting for the newly formed Fort Assinniboine Preservation Association.

"Sometimes it's hard to know how to answer questions," he says. "The tourists always want to know why the fort was built here in the first place. The standard answer is that it was built to protect the settlers from the Indians. I never feel comfortable saying that, especially when Indians are along on the tour."

"The Indians are interested in the fort?"

"Some have been."

He has already led me through the handful of surviving buildings—the old guardhouse, shops and stables, carriage houses, one of the officers' quarters—and told me about the preservation association's hopes for their renovation. Then we hiked down the hill toward Beaver Creek on two dusty ruts, past the traces of those massive root cellars and ice cellars that once supplied five hundred troops. Now he parts the knee-deep grass on the old parade grounds to show me traces of cement crumbling into the sod. A sidewalk once kept a general's feet out of the trampled mud when he wanted to walk from the officers' quarters on one side of the fort to the barracks on the other.

I feel as though I've seen enough deteriorating brick. The surviving buildings are claustrophobic, characterless, utilitarian with no further use. What, I wonder, could all this dusty space be renovated into? What theme would it illustrate? Compared with Fort Assinniboine, Fort Mcleod on the Canadian side of the border looks like a movie set with its sharpened pole palisades and log bastions. A movie about the War of American Independence, perhaps, in the kind of fort Simon Girty might have betrayed to the British, or Betty Zane might have run to save. Fort Mcleod's pine bark and smell of fresh resin recall an earlier frontier, an innocence of sabers in the path of a juggernaut, a storybook fort in the shadow of a modern military installation. Our dream of capturing that innocence for ourselves, it seems to me, would have been a likelier motive for invasion than any dream of empire.

Trees have been planted on the fort grounds since the old days, tall papery cottonwoods and the hardy gray Russian olives. From here I cannot see the butte where the Indians fired down at the soldiers that first day and led them to expect bloodier conflict in the days to come. But I remember Nicholas Hardeman's conclusion, that the sheer size and presence of Fort Assinniboine, its show of strength, was what steered Montana's northern plains from turbulence to tranquility.

The plains do seem quiet these days, to say the least. Here on the vanished parade grounds of Fort Assinniboine, where a lawn sprinkler sweeps the small patch of green grass around the open windows of a surviving brick house, where a secretary for the Montana State University Experiment Station taps at a word processor, who could guess the military presence, silent and far deadlier than Black Jack Pershing and his Buffalo soldiers ever dreamed, of the MX missile silos that ring the prairie? The MX missiles, too, are said to show strength.

My friend and I drift into talk about Havre, the railroad town that replaced the old whiskey settlement of Bullhook Bottoms north of the fort, and about the changes that have come about since I taught at the college there. Montana's tax base, heavily dependent upon agriculture and energy, has been badly eroded by the years of drought and plummeting prices of oil and natural gas and corresponding depletion of its population. Highways deteriorate, state institutions have been cut back, businesses have closed. Trying to imagine the future, remembering the old paranoia that spewed from the local newspapers when the Rocky Boy Reservation was established, I think I understand another of our reasons for the fort and perhaps for the missiles.

"You were lucky to leave the Highline when you did," my friend says.

"What about you? Will you stay here?"

But he is noncommittal. He speaks of his work, of his love for local history. His gaze wanders across the dense grass, and I

follow his gaze to the weed growth that marks the old foundations. I am teased by the interest of local Indians in the old fort.
I wonder what they see in the crumbling bricks. If it were left to
them, would they renovate Fort Assinniboine or raze it?

But here in the sunlight, among the bobbing seed heads,
under the enormous white floating cumuli, I feel the prairie's
insistence. With good rain this summer, with the chance for a
good wheat crop in the fall, surely another year is possible. We're
not finished here yet.

Mother Lode

ER PARENTS HAD LEFT MINNESOTA AND COME TO
Big Sandy, Montana, in 1889 to look for ranchland.
They brought the girl, Bertha, with them. She was
eighteen. Probably she resented being dragged along. The high
northern plains would have seemed like the end of the earth to
her. Years later, in a novel called *The Lonesome Trail*, she
described the landscape as "great, gray plains . . . scarred and
broken with sharp-nosed hills and deep, water-worn coulees
gleaming barren and yellow in the sun."

Her family had come to Big Sandy, as it turned out, during
a stasis in its history. For centuries the northern plains had been
the territory of the Blackfeet Indians, but by 1889 the Blackfeet
had been driven west in one sad retreat after another to a fragment of their old lands. In another twenty years the Enlarged
Homestead Act would bring settlers by the hundreds and thousands to northern Montana to try their luck homesteading on
320 dryland acres.

But in 1889 Big Sandy, Montana, was the hub of the last of
the great unfenced cattle empires. Across these gray hills—"these
thousand hills," as A. B. Guthrie, Jr., later called them—the
drama of trail drives, of spring and fall roundups, of bucking

horses and range wars and cattle rustlers and vigilantes and, most of all, cowboys—was playing itself out as though twilight had not fallen upon the open cattle range as surely as it had upon the Blackfeet.

Its twilight lasted quite a while. In fact, the North Montana Roundup Association would continue to wield political power along the Milk River until well past the turn of the century, and a few open-range cattle operations would hang on along the river breaks through the 1920s. But whether the girl, Bertha Muzzy, was struck at once by cowboy glamour and tales of the glory days is unclear. What mainly was on her mind in 1889 was how to get away from her parents.

The year after she came to northern Montana, nineteen-year-old Bertha married a neighboring rancher named Clayton Jay Bower. Bower was much older than Bertha, and, according to old Highline gossip, had had a long and perfectly satisfactory marriage until Bertha broke it up. Whatever the truth of that allegation, there she was—a ranch wife. She and Clayton Jay Bower had two sons and a daughter in quick order. But still young Bertha was discontented.

About the same time that Bertha and Clayton Jay Bower were ranching in the Milk River valley, another young woman was raising her children and coping with the hardships of ranch life south of Miles City, Montana. In *A Bride Goes West*, Nannie Alderson remembered, "I don't think there is anyone so unfitted to raise children as a tired mother, and I was always tired. And then too there were the effects of isolation and of living inside four walls. . . . There were weeks, in our long winters, when I scarcely left the house, except to hang clothes on the line."

But if Bertha Muzzy Bower felt isolated and frantic and exhausted during the 1890s, she left no such reminiscences. Instead, she began writing, in longhand on a kitchen table, a novel about a ranch she called the Flying U, near a small north Montana town she called Dry Lake.

How did this young woman with three small children, a

spotty education, and few resources turn to writing, and why? How did she find the minutes, or hours? Was she creating "psychic space" for herself, as Carolyn Heilbrun has described her own foray into detective fiction? Was the drive, as some late-twentieth-century women have said of themselves, to weave a web of words against the threat of annihilation, against the great gray empty outdoors? Or was the dreaming, perhaps, of another kind of freedom? Of her own money, earned by her own writing?

Whatever the case, Bertha Muzzy Bower saw her first novel, *Chip of the Flying U*, serialized by the publishers Street and Smith in 1904. *Chip of the Flying U* was so successful that G. W. Dillingham brought it out in hardcover, and Bertha's subsequent life reads like the fantasies of women writing in longhand on kitchen tables everywhere—well, it does if you gloss over the failed marriages, the disappointments, the ups and downs of a writer's life.

She divorced Clayton Jay Bower, married a second time, and went off to California to become a professional writer. Apparently all she took with her was the name Bower, which everyone, including her own children, called her for the rest of her life. As B. M. Bower she bore another daughter, divorced and remarried and divorced once more, and published sixty-eight novels, over a hundred short stories, and a lot of screenplays. Many of her novels were adapted for the screen. *Chip of the Flying U* was filmed four times.

Chip of the Flying U has been compared, since it first appeared, with Owen Wister's *The Virginian*, which was published two years earlier, in 1902. Maybe B. M. Bower had read *The Virginian* and thought to tap into its success. Both novels are light and often comic in tone; both describe working cattle ranches and the conflicts between eastern expectations and western codes; both center on a romance between a cowboy and an educated, privileged eastern woman. And yet *Chip* and *The Virginian* are enormously different.

Violence in *The Virginian* includes murder, beatings (human and animal), the capture and hanging of cattle rustlers, and the prototype of all western gun duels in the main street of town, complete with the prototype of all schoolmarms: If you do face Trampas and gun him down, she tells the Virginian, "there can be no to-morrow for you and me." The action of *Chip of the Flying U*, on the other hand, includes nothing worse than a practical joke that gets out of hand, a pack of obnoxious children who get their stomachs pumped out by the heroine (and serves them right, too), and an outlaw horse that throws himself over backward on Chip and damages him badly enough for the heroine to doctor him. The only death is that of a coyote, shot by the heroine.

The action of *The Virginian* is viewed through the eyes of a visiting easterner, who looks for and finds the romance of the West. *Chip of the Flying U*, in contrast, is told from the point of view of an omniscient author who sees the ordinary, day-to-day West. No mistake here: B. M. Bower may have wanted a piece of the success of *The Virginian*, but she also knew her cattle frontier. "There's more of loneliness and monotony in pioneering than there is of battle," she wrote in 1924. "I can personally vouch for the fact that pioneering was—and still is—about ninety per cent monotonous isolation to ten per cent thrill. It is scarcely fair to turn the picture upside down and present the public with ninety per cent thrill and ten per cent normal, everyday living."

Fairness may be B. M. Bower's smokescreen for what she really wanted to write about. She could turn out thrillers when she wanted to, or when she wanted the money, but in fact she was far more interested in daily ranch life than she was in superimposed dime-novel adventure. And so, where *The Virginian* is romantic, *Chip of the Flying U* seems dusty and realistic.

I remember being amazed by Bower's realism the first time I read *Chip*. I was ten years old and had dragged a faded hardcover copy at random from the shelves of the old Carnegie library in Lewistown, Montana, where Bower's novels lived beside those of Zane Grey and countless other forgotten western genre novels. My first response, as I burrowed into the pages, was to fall in love with Chip. My second was a genuine epiphany, which I shouted aloud—"Hey! The man in this book is reading the *Great Falls Tribune!*"

Until then, it had never dawned on me that the place where I lived could be the setting for fiction, or familiar day-to-day details the substance of fiction. Romance, I had always believed, lay out there in the vast elsewhere, and I understood, without knowing I understood, that the power of story *was to give to airy nothing / a local habitation and a name.* What I had read about up until then—gunfights, abductions, Indian raids, and lynchings —existed in a way that my daytime world, uninvented, un-written about, did not exist. Now I absorbed Bower's minutiae of day-to-day ranch life. I couldn't get enough.

The cowboys of the Flying U's Happy Family—and Bower went on to write many more Happy Family novels—are first introduced when Shorty brings a letter out to the ranch for the Old Man, James G. Whitmore. Bower takes time to draw attention to a detail which, for her characters, is much too ordinary to take notice of, but which I, as a ten-year-old reader, seized upon as absolutely accurate. The way a horse will startle at trivia had been drilled into me—*never wave paper at a horse*—and to this day I remember the effect that Bower's description had on me as clearly as I now read about the effect of a fluttering white envelope on a cow horse.

> James G. stood in the path, waving a square envelope aloft before Shorty, who regarded it with supreme indifference.
>
> Not so Shorty's horse. He rolled his eyes till the whites showed, snorted and backed away from the fluttering white object.
>
> "Doggone it, where's this been?" reiterated James G., accusingly.
>
> "How the devil do I know?" retorted Shorty, forcing his horse nearer. "In the office, most likely. I got it with the rest today."

"It's two weeks old," stormed the Old Man. "I never knew it to fail—if a letter says anybody's coming, or you're to hurry up and go somewhere to meet somebody, that letter's the one that monkeys around and comes when the last dog's hung."

The letter, of course, announces the imminent visit of James G.'s sister, Dell Whitmore, who has, of all things in 1904, just graduated from medical school. Chip, the misogynist cowboy, is sent to Dry Lake to meet her train, but not before the cowboys speculate on what kind of a woman Dell might be—"a skinny old maid with a peaked nose and glasses," they decide, and they plot a fake lynching to fulfill what they suppose will be her expectations of the West.

Alas, it is the cowboys' expectations that are heightened, then dashed. Dell, the Little Doctor, turns out to be young, pretty, and as level-headed as one might expect of a medical school graduate. Far from fainting at the sound of gunfire, or even indulging in a lecture on nonviolence, she astonishes Chip on the drive back to the ranch by shooting a coyote and then analyzing its carcass. "Look, here's where I hit him the first time; the bullet took a diagonal course from the shoulder back to the other side. It must have gone within an inch of his heart, and would have finished him in a short time, without that other shot—that penetrated his brain, you see; death was instantaneous." And she quickly sizes up the "lynching" that greets her arrival at the ranch and plays along with it. "Hurry up," she commands, "so I can be in at the death. Remember, I'm a doctor."

B. M. Bower certainly was aware of the conventions of the western romance tradition she was invading. Chip himself mutters about western romances that get the facts wrong and assume that bronc-busters never take off their spurs. When, laid up with his dislocated ankle, bored from inactivity, he appropriates Dell's oils and brushes and paints over her sentimental treatment of a Missouri breaks landscape, he replaces her inauthentic and prettified scenery with "dirty gray snow drifts, where a chinook had cut them, and icy side hills. . . . A poor, half-starved range cow with her calf which the round-up had overlooked in the fall, stood at bay against a steep cut bank. Before them squatted five great, gaunt wolves."

Bower's description of Chip's painting is, in fact, a description of a painting called *The Last Stand*, by a friend of hers, the cowboy artist Charles M. Russell, who illustrated the first hardcover edition of *Chip of the Flying U* for her. Bower's commitment to Russell's brand of western realism, to his exactitude and faithfulness to detail, is obvious. But could she have been going further? Could she have been deliberately parodying the romantic western convention, and, in particular, *The Virginian*?

A famous and funny scene in *The Virginian* occurs during a dance at a ranch house, when the cowboys slip into a bedroom and switch the sleeping babies in their blankets—and no one notices the switch until the parents have driven home with the wrong babies. Their mothers (although not their fathers) are furious, and they confront the cowboys in an uproar. In a long aftermath, the Virginian and the schoolmarm debate western versus eastern standards of behavior: spontaneity versus propriety, openness versus hypocrisy, the natural versus the civilized, the masculine verses the feminine.

A scene in *Chip of the Flying U* also includes a ranch dance, and children and cowboys and an eastern woman, but with the difference that east-west, male-female collaboration, not the collision of their values, is its point.

While their parents are dancing in the next room, the neighborhood "holy terrors" have invaded the Little Doctor's office, unlocked her drug cabinet, and sampled her "candy." A stomach pump is called for.

> "I'm going to use this." The Little Doctor held up a fearsome thing to view. "Open your mouth, Josephine."
>
> Josephine refused; her refusal was emphatic and unequivocal, punctuated by sundry kicks directed at whoever came within range of her stout little shoes.
>
> "Here's where we shine," broke in a cheery voice which was

sweet to the ears, just then. "Chip and I ain't wrassled with bronks all our lives for nothing. This is dead easy—all same branding calves. Ketch hold of her heels, Splinter . . ."

It did not take long—as Weary had said, it was very much like branding calves. No sooner was one child made to disgorge and laid, limp and subdued upon the bed, than Chip and Weary seized another dexterously by heels and head.

Is this parody? It is tempting to imagine that young woman writing with her pencil and her tablet at her kitchen table, yearning for success in *The Virginian*'s tradition but at the same time longing to puncture its assumptions. Certainly if, as Jane Tomkins believes, *The Virginian* is a reaction against a female-dominated tradition of popular culture, then *Chip of the Flying U* is a reconciliation of male and female, of east and west. It is a comedy that treats the age-old theme of the tension between the sexes and ends with its resolution.

Dell, the Little Doctor, is attractive because she is competent and self-possessed, and because she has a sense of proportion. She never has to sacrifice her dignity or "stoop" to conquer; she neither flaunts her medical degree nor devalues it. Of the Montana State Medical Board, she remarks, "They were awfully nice to me—they seemed to think a girl doctor is some kind of joke out here. They didn't make it any easier, though; they acted as if they didn't expect me to pass—but I did!" And as he reads her license to practice medicine, her brother, endearingly "growing prouder every line," replies, "You're all right, Dell—I'll be doggoned if you ain't."

And Chip—why is Chip so attractive? Is it because, to paraphrase the title of Pam Houston's *Cowboys Are My Weakness*, a cowboy is every bookish girl's fantasy?

The reason, I think, is also the main reason for the deep differences between *The Virginian*, which is a male fantasy of the West, and *Chip of the Flying U*, which is a female fantasy tempered with firsthand experience. (Not that their readers ever seem to divide along gender lines; I loved *The Virginian* as a child, and I know grown men who speak fondly of their early reading with the Flying U bunch and of their assumptions that B. M. Bower was a man.) Bertha Muzzy Bower, dreaming at her kitchen table, must have decided that if she was going to fantasize herself up a cowboy, she might as well fantasize one she liked. Certainly *not* the Virginian, who would bore any girl with his rhapsodizing and drive her wild with his moralizing and his insistence on having his own way.

No. Let us have a good-looking young man who may be aloof—we'll cure him of that—but also gifted and decent, and good at what he does. He'll be certain enough of himself to change his mind about eastern women and to be unthreatened by a professional one; he's only a little anxious about social status and uncertain enough to fear the arrival in Dry Lake, Montana, of one Dr. Cecil Granthum of Gilroy, Ohio. He feels called upon to be masterful only where it counts: in the clinch.

As a reviewer from Brooklyn wrote in 1906, "'Chip' is all right. Better than 'The Virginian.'"

Born in Iowa in 1905, Dorothy Marie Johnson was seven years old when her parents moved to the little railroad town of Whitefish, Montana. In March 1913, when a sleepy Dorothy and her parents, carrying her and their suitcases, stepped off the train, Whitefish was far from the mecca it has become for skiers, movie stars, and investors in mountain-view and lakeside property. "Whitefish was a child of the late frontier, still being hacked out of the woods. We were kids together," Dorothy Johnson remembered in her memoir, *When You and I Were Young, Whitefish*. "I was a nice little girl. The town was a sturdy, brawling, mannerless brat that took years to civilize."

Whitefish is only a few hours' train ride from Big Sandy, Montana (or at least, it used to be, before the railroad spurs shrank back into fewer and fewer main lines), on the old Empire Builder, along the Great Northern's original Highline, to distinguish it from its southern, or lower, line. Unlike Big Sandy, which was the hub of the cattle frontier, Whitefish started as a logging settlement on the site of an old Indian encampment and became a railroad town. In 1904, James J. Hill had made Whitefish a division point for the Great Northern, with a roundhouse, switch yards, repair facilities, and headquarters for permanent employees, and the tradition continues. Today the engineers and brakemen of the Burlington Northern line still rumble back and forth along the Highline, and local jokes abound about the wife in Whitefish and the girlfriend in Havre, or maybe it's the other way around.

Where Big Sandy sleeps in the heart of gray prairie with its cutbanks and cloud shadows and wind and dust, Whitefish spreads along the shores of a long, narrow lake embedded in the northern Rockies. Trees cover those mountains. Quaking aspens live their short lives of fifty years or so in the valleys and on the lower slopes, their pale green leaves trembling among the darker firs and through the stumps that mark old clearcuts. The giant Balm of Gilead, or western balsam poplar, smells of spice in the spring and oozes resin as the weather warms. Cottonwoods hold to the river bottoms, as do the many species of willows. Higher on the slopes, lodgepole pines follow the fireweed and the aspen in growing over burned areas and clearcuts. White pine and balsam fir grow up to the timberline, becoming stunted but sweet-smelling the higher they climb. Ponderosa pine, yellow pine, juniper, Douglas fir, Engelmann spruce—all the evergreens in shades of dark green, all the beautiful names.

Whitefish was a paradise for children. With the neighborhood boys, Dorothy played and explored, built tepees and imagined herself a conquering Indian chieftain or a cowboy in a war with the nesters. She went huckleberrying, fishing, camping, hunting. After her father died (she was only ten) she pitched in to help her mother make ends meet and to save money for college. Odd jobs, errand-running, gardening, selling subscriptions, selling homemade horseradish, helping with the great annual

Whitefish tin-can-cleanup campaign, and finally, the job as a relief switchboard operator in the Whitefish telephone office which she held through high school and which, years later, provided her with the material for "Confessions of a Telephone Girl." It was as if she knew she had to hit life at a run, because she never slowed down.

She read everything she could get her hands on, worrying her mother that she would go blind. Photographs of her as a child show her peering through thick, rimless glasses with the characteristic tilt of her head and the smile hiding in the corner of her mouth that stayed with her the rest of her life. Most of the time she wore starched dresses and hair bows that belied the tomboy under the surface, but on her mountain outings it was men's bib overalls and a floppy hat. In 1918 she started her freshman year at Central High School in Whitefish, and did she ever love the drama club and the debate club and her work on the yearbook, although she found Latin "gruesome" and science even worse. Four years later (she was only sixteen) she graduated high school, second in a class of fourteen. Then, *then*, it was off to the state college in Bozeman for Dorothy, where she signed up for pre-med because, she said, she had read *Chip of the Flying U* when she was twelve and had been so taken by the Little Doctor, who had won the heart of Chip. She didn't stick long with the pre-med program—"I wasn't doing very well in qualitative analysis. . . . Besides, the cat course was coming up the next year. I couldn't see myself cutting up a cat, especially when you had to get the cat."

And so the next year, she transferred to the university in Missoula, where she majored in English and met H. G. Merriam, the professor who had been a Rhodes scholar in Oxford, who had founded a literary magazine, *The Frontier*, and who fostered the teaching of creative writing in Montana. He mentored A. B. Guthrie, Jr., Dan Cushman, Grace Stone Coates, Gwendolyn Haste, D'Arcy McNickle. Dorothy, determined now to become a writer, couldn't have been more fortunate. She began to submit her poems to Merriam, to become a part of his select group of students.

Like Dorothy Johnson, I enrolled in creative writing courses at the University of Montana well before the famous MFA in creative writing existed. At that time, during the late 1950s and early 1960s, my professors impressed on me that the most important writer in the Rocky Mountain West was Walter Van Tilburg Clark, who recently had left Montana to teach in Nevada and write *The City of Trembling Leaves*. We students all read "The Indian Well" and "The Winds and Snows of Winter" and "The Portable Phonograph," along with a lot of Hemingway, and I understood very clearly what other people thought fiction should be about.

A Katherine Anne Porter story, "The Grave," was included in the anthology for one of our creative writing classes. The instructor said that Porter didn't show him much, because she wrote about birthing and such, of interest only to women. I thought the instructor was stupid, and before the class was over, I imagine he thought I was obnoxious. But I was never fully aware that I was going along with an assumption that writing was something that belonged to men and their interests, and I was completely unaware of how that unquestioned assumption was limiting me. I was writing a lot of tough rural stuff, using a male point of view, and one of my professors advised me to submit my stories to literary quarterlies under a man's name.

After I left the University of Montana, I heard stories about the macho atmosphere during the early years when Richard Hugo and William Kittredge taught in the creative writing program. In his memoir *Hole in the Sky*, Kittredge tells a story from those days that has become a legend:

> Our first day in Missoula . . . I went unannounced to introduce myself to the main writer in town, the poet Richard Hugo. I marched onto the concrete porch of his little house above the downtown fishing waters where Rattlesnake Creek flows into the

Clark Fork River, and rapped a few times. Nothing. I rapped again. Hugo opened the door, a heavy unshaven man in a paint-stained sweatshirt. He studied me like an anthropologist, squinting his eyes. "You're very drunk," he said.

Here, I thought, now you've done it.

"I'll join you," he said.

Maybe this was home.

"That story went through the department like wildfire," said a woman who was enrolled in the creative writing program at the time. "And all the guys were like, *Yes! These are real writers! Aren't they wonderful!* But not all of us thought their bar-crawling was so wonderful."

The scene at the Eastgate Tavern, the tough talk, the condescension in seminars, and the assumption, perhaps, that certain subject matter simply wasn't accessible to women? Later I thought that the reason why Montana women of my generation weren't writing fiction was because they had been unable to find their own stories within the dominating western mythology of solitude, questing, conflict, and destruction. And unlike Dorothy Johnson a generation earlier, we weren't interested in appropriating the western myth for ourselves.

So she was fortunate in being mentored by H. G. Merriam, but in other respects, Dorothy was unlucky in Missoula. She was attending classes and washing dishes to make ends meet, she was so sick and worried about her mother, who was sick at home in Whitefish, that she developed a tremor and finally broke down. She left the university and went back to Whitefish for a while, tried normal school, tried business school, worked in Spokane and Seattle and in Whitefish again. But she kept sending H. G. Merriam her poems, and eventually she came back to Missoula, switched from writing poems to short stories, finished her degree in English (she was still only twenty-one), and married a gambler named Red Peterkin.

What is it about bookish girls and the wrong men? Dorothy

had mistaken Red Peterkin for Chip, and it was a bad mistake. She and Red lived together in Missoula for only a few months before she took a job as a stenographer in the little reservation town of Okanagan, in northern Washington. After a while he followed her to Okanagan, spent a winter with her, and ran up sizable debts. And then he left her. She never saw him again. She did pay his debts. On her tombstone is carved *Paid in Full.*

And that was that. Except, of course, for the rest of her life. Dorothy M. Johnson moved from Okanagan to New York, worked as a magazine editor, and began to hit the big markets with her short stories. After fifteen years she went back to Whitefish as a newspaperwoman, continuing to turn out those spare, thrilling western stories, and after that she moved to Missoula and became secretary-manager of the Montana State Press Association, with a courtesy title of assistant professor of journalism at the University of Montana. Like Whitefish, Missoula is set in the mountains. Dorothy Johnson always loved the mountains; she said they protected her from whatever was out there.

Along with countless poems, articles, and essays, she wrote fifty-two short stories and seventeen full-length books. Her novel *Buffalo Woman* won her the Western Heritage Wrangler Award for the outstanding western novel of 1978; her stories "Lost Sister" and "A Man Called Horse" went into *The Western Hall of Fame*; the Western Writers of America gave her their Levi Strauss Golden Saddleman Award for her contributions to the history and legends of the West. The motion picture based on her story "The Man Who Shot Liberty Valance," starring John Wayne, James Stewart, and Lee Marvin, can be found in the classic western section of the video stores. Gary Cooper and Maria Schell starred in *The Hanging Tree*, based on Dorothy's novella, and Richard Harris and Judith Anderson in *A Man Called Horse*, which Shana Alexander called the most authentic Indian movie ever filmed, but which Dorothy despised for, among other sins, changing her Northern Cheyenne characters into Sioux. Of all Montana writers, Dorothy M. Johnson and A. B. Guthrie, Jr., are the most distinguished and acclaimed. They are among the most distinguished and acclaimed writers in the West.

What did she write about, this serious girl, who grew square and stocky, who kept both feet on the ground and wore her white hair in a rigid set, but never lost the glint behind the eyeglasses? This woman who, after that disastrous early marriage, remained single and worked for the rest of her life as though she were being driven?

As B. M. Bower had done, Dorothy Johnson appropriated the materials of western mythology. She wrote about the cowboys, the pioneers, the gamblers, the fortune seekers, the gunslingers, and she did it with an elegance that led some reviewers to compare her style with Hemingway's. Where her contemporary, A. B. Guthrie, Jr., was preoccupied with the death of landscape, Dorothy Johnson was far more interested in people, in valiant action and sacrifice and lost causes, and she wrote in the western genre better than any other western genre writer, before or since. Her comic-contemporary Beulah Bunny stories appeared in the *Saturday Evening Post* during the 1940s, and she brought out her first collection, *Indian Country*, in 1947, the same year that A. B. Guthrie, Jr., published *The Big Sky*. Like *The Big Sky*, *Indian Country* was heralded for its authenticity and integrity. "Here is no glamorizing, no romantic gilding, of settlers or of Indians," wrote Jack Schafer, author of *Shane*, in his introduction to *Indian Country*.

Bower's novels are told in third person and usually set in the gritty present. Many of Dorothy Johnson's stories are told from the point of view of an omniscient narrator who looks back from a far vantage point with wistfulness into the distant past. *Forty years later*, begins the final paragraph of "Flame on the Frontier." *Twelve years later*, begins the final paragraph of "Prairie Kid." *Bert Barricune was my friend for more than thirty years*, explains the senator in "The Man Who Shot Liberty Valance." *Fifty years later, the evil he had meant to do still plagued him*, concludes "The Man Who Knew the Buckskin Kid." *Latigo is dead long years ago*, remembers Grandma Foster in "Laugh in the Face of Danger." The action of these stories is irrevocably past, lost, almost forgotten, perhaps retained only in the memories of the secretive or the senile, but all the more precious for its precariousness. These are stories about courage, Dorothy Johnson said, which she wrote because she lacked courage, herself.

They are also about loss. Grandma Foster in "Laugh in the Face of Danger" married a good man and raised a family, but in her old age longs for the outlaw Latigo Randy. "'We went to New Mexico,' she said hoarsely. 'Him and me together. Rode at night, hid by day.' Oh, that must have been the way it was!" Hallie in "The Man Who Shot Liberty Valance" marries the senator but strews prickly-pear blossoms on Bert Barricune's coffin. Aunt Bessie in "Lost Sister" gives up her life as a decoy for her half-Indian son. In "The Last Boast," Wolfer Joe abandons the girl who would have ridden away with him; hanged for murder fourteen years later, he leaves a friend "puzzling about how betraying a woman could be a thing a man might boast of with the last words he ever had a chance to speak."

Often the conclusions of her stories are disturbing, none more so than in "Flame on the Frontier," where Sara, who was captured by Indians as a child and ransomed as a young woman, is slapped by her husband for talking to an Indian who once courted her. "As she went down to the spring for a bucket of water, she was singing. . . . She had two crying children and was pregnant again. But two men loved her, and both of them had just proved it."

"How could she write that?" I asked a friend who had known Dorothy Johnson.

"I asked her that, once," he said.

"What did she say?"

"She said, *Oh, you know how love is.*"

A Monte Dolack painting shows the elderly Dorothy Johnson at her manual typewriter. Her white hair is set in its rigid waves. She wears a sedate dark blue dress with a white collar. She would look like a retired schoolteacher except for her necklace of bear claws and the way her eyes glint through her glasses.

Behind her in the painting, looming up as though from her imagination, are John Wayne, Lee Marvin, James Stewart, and Gary Cooper as they appeared in movies based on her stories. And I long to ask her what she's doing in that company. Why did she write within the conventions of genre fiction, why did she set such stern limitations upon herself? Why was courage, for her, a thing of the past? Did she yearn for Chip of the Flying U all her life? I don't know what she'd say.

Oh, you know how love is.

Mildred Walker also was born in 1905, in Philadelphia. Her father was a Baptist minister and her mother was a teacher, and while they probably had as little money as B. M. Bower's or Dorothy Johnson's family, they did bring Mildred up under considerably more genteel circumstances and with higher aspirations. She attended Wells College and graduated magna cum laude, and then she married a young doctor, Ferdinand Ripley Schemm (ironic how the medical profession runs like a thread through these women's lives) and lived with him on the Upper Peninsula of Michigan for several years, where he practiced among the loggers and their families. She earned an M.A. in creative writing and won the Avery Hopwood Award for her first novel, *Fireweed*. A later novel, *The Body of a Young Man*, would be nominated for a National Book Award, and another, *Southwest Corner*, would be made into a Broadway play.

And so it was as a doctor's wife and an established novelist that Mildred Walker, in 1933, came to Great Falls, Montana, which her husband had chosen as the place where he could best continue his research. The doctor's wife entered into the life of the community, joining the Junior League, selling tickets to the state fair, helping with charities, socializing. The novelist went on writing (she wrote nine of her thirteen novels in Montana), but so unobtrusively that many of her friends were completely unaware of what she was doing. Her daughter, the poet Ripley Schemm, says she was ten years old before she realized that her mother was writing novels. It was as if she were two women: Mrs. Ferdinand Schemm, who observed the proprieties, wore white gloves to teas, and dressed her three children as formally as little royals; and Mildred Walker, who wrote novels about young women who chafed at restraints and conventions.

But she had not lived in Montana long before she paid a visit to the only bookstore in Great Falls—the Book and Gift— and asked, with quiet courtesy, whether the proprietor might not consider displaying her books.

"Oh! You're an author?" said the proprieter. "Why, we've got another author right back here, browsing. You've got to meet him!"

It was Joseph Kinsey Howard, the bearlike newspaperman from Great Falls, who at that time was collecting material for his influential anthology, *Montana Margins*, and who would go on to write a history of the state called *Montana: High, Wide and Handsome* and a history of Louis Riel and the Métis called *Strange Empire.*

Joe Howard looked at the doctor's wife.

"I never read women's fiction," he said.

An annoying thing about anecdotes is the way they end, as though what Joe Howard said to Mildred Walker matters more than what she said back to him. Whatever she said, their encounter turned out to be the beginning of a twenty-year friendship between Howard and the Schemms. Their friendship eventually expanded to include A. B. Guthrie, Jr., and flowered through long summers in neighboring cabins originally built by Métis settlers in a mountain canyon west of Choteau, Montana.

It was the most improbable of writers' circles. Mildred Walker, Joseph Kinsey Howard, and A. B. Guthrie, Jr. The men were at work reinterpreting the past. Guthrie was at work on his cycle of novels on the doomed West. He said he wanted to replace the glossed-over treatment of the West with "the rough, tough, sinful, brave-heroic aspect" of the frontier, but what he achieved was a fantasy of escape from civilization into unspoiled, untouched wilderness where white men could act on impulse and live without restraint or rules. Howard was writing the history of Montana as a conflict between civilization and the frontier, between cynicism and idealism, between the eastern banking establishment and western independence, all staged against a beautiful landscape of rich natural resources that, from the beginning of white settlement, had been abused and exploited by pressures from "outside." He was researching one of the great forgotten romances, one of the lost causes of all time in the history and culture of the Métis, in particular the two rebellions led by their fanatical leader, Louis Riel, against Canada, through which the half-breeds and their Cree allies hoped to carve an independent native state called Assiniboia out of present-day Saskatchewan.

Given the time and the place and the friendship, anyone might have expected Mildred Walker to follow this blazed trail. Like Howard and Guthrie and Dorothy Johnson, she might have used her skills to polish and hone and to reinvest in the old myth of the West as paradise before the fall. But she did nothing of the kind.

Only one of Mildred Walker's thirteen novels (*If a Lion Could Talk*, 1970) is set in the Montana past, and its vision of the wilderness has more in common with the psychological horrors plumbed by Joseph Conrad, whose *Heart of Darkness* Mildred Walker was teaching at the time, than with *The Big Sky*'s romantic fantasy of escape from civilization and responsibility. The plot of *If a Lion Could Talk* has to do with a young missionary couple, Mark and Harriet Ryegate, who are sponsored by a Baptist church in Massachusetts to travel to the Montana Territory in about 1856 to convert the Blackfeet Indians to Christianity. As Harriet travels by steamboat up the Missouri River to join her husband in Fort Benton, she writes in her journal about her growing aversion to the landscape.

> I wish we were on the sea instead of this endless river. It has turned shallow in places and the crew have to pull the boat by ropes from the shore. They look like slaves, all tied to a rope, half-naked, cursing, straining till you can see the muscles in their bodies bulge. Just now we went between high clay banks, higher than my window, that made my room so dark I felt I was being buried alive. I rushed out on the deck to escape.

In Fort Benton the Ryegates are offered the hospitality of Major Phillips and his beautiful Blackfeet wife, Eenisskim (based on the historical Major Culbertson and his Indian wife, Natawista), but they cannot make connections with the people they have come to minister to. The Indians laugh at Mark's sermons, and he becomes convinced that the French Canadian clerk at the fort who serves as his translator is twisting his words. Mark is certain that he could win Indian converts to Protestant Christianity if only he could persuade Eenisskim to translate for him. But Eenisskim refuses to speak English, although she understands it very well. She laughs at Mark and teases him as he grows more and more obsessed with her. One of Mark's most profound wilderness experiences, when he naps on a river bank and dreams of being lifted to heaven on an eagle's wings, turns out to be a prank of Eenisskim's, holding a wet duck over him as he sleeps.

Later, Mark tries and fails to comfort Eenisskim when her son drowns and she isolates herself on a remote butte to hack off her hair, slash her arms, smear herself with ashes, and howl her grief. She ignores Mark, whose faith in himself is shaken when he realizes that he loves her with a love she cannot feel. Mark uses Harriet's pregnancy as an excuse to slink back to Massachusetts, where he tries to return to his old pulpit. But both Ryegates have been disillusioned with themselves and with each other. Their experience of the wilderness has not been of paradise before the fall but of mankind unredeemed, and their task for the rest of the novel is to accept and try to transcend the ugliness of their own souls.

But the two Montana novels of Mildred Walker's that I dug out of the high school library shelves when I was fifteen and realized as I read that my place and my experiences were valid subjects for a writer were *Winter Wheat* (1944) and *The Curlew's Cry* (1955). *Winter Wheat* is the better known of the two novels—it was a Literary Guild selection in 1944—and it was my favorite. I identified intensely with Ellen Webb, the girl who grows up on a dryland wheat ranch in north-central Montana, goes away to college at the beginning of World War II, and eventually returns to the home ranch, which has become a psychological battle-ground between her aesthetic, Vermont-bred father and her tough, unsentimental Russian mother. I admired Ellen's compe-tence, and I understood her attachment to her parents, her ambivalence about the harsh, beautiful landscape of her child-hood, and her longing to break boundaries and see more of the world than fields and sky, grain elevators and unpainted farm buildings. Especially her longing! To get away, to read and learn, to see what the world holds—why, why, does she have to leave college and go home? Will she ever go back? Surely, in her pain over the fiancé from the East who had jilted her because he couldn't see marrying a woman stronger than himself, she won't marry a jerk and settle down to raise his children.

I hated so many of the books recommended for high school girls' reading, which were about young women with high aspi-rations who had to learn to settle for less. Their parents needed them, or younger brothers and sisters needed them, or some-body needed them; any old reason was good enough for sacrifice and self-abnegation, it seemed to me. Fortunately, the conclu-sion to *Winter Wheat* is sufficiently open-ended to imagine any number of choices for Ellen. And its language rang for me then as it does now, reminding me of the beauty in the commonplace as Ellen listens to a report of wheat prices on the radio.

> "One heavy dark Northern Spring . . . fifty-two." The words came so fast they seemed to roll downhill. Nobody ever calls it all that; it's just spring wheat, but I like the words. They heap up and make a picture of a spring that's slow to come, when the ground stays frozen late into March and the air is raw, and the skies are sulky and dark. The "Northern" makes me feel how close we are to the Rockies and how high up on the map, almost to Canada.
> "One dark hard Winter . . . fifty-three."

The Curlew's Cry, on the other hand, was published in the same year that Mildred Walker's husband died. It is about a small-town Montana girl who graduates from high school in the fictional Brandon Rapids in 1905, leaves home briefly for a short, sad marriage to a wealthy man in the East, and returns to Brandon Rapids to live out her life. Pamela Lacey is bright, evasive, lonely, brought up in the openness of the West, fiercely loyal to her heritage, and yet full of doubts about that heritage as it seems to stifle her ambitions. At fifteen I was disturbed by Pamela and her choices, which I thought Mildred Walker was forcing upon her. Rereading *The Curlew's Cry* recently, I experienced the sensation of double vision that many readers feel when they return to old favorites. Pamela Lacey is still Pamela, bright, evasive, and lonely, and I am still her partisan; but while I can clearly remember my indignation at age fifteen at the conclusion of the novel, I am no longer certain that Mildred Walker allows Pamela less from life than Pamela can claim.

In *The Curlew's Cry*, Mildred Walker anticipates many of the themes—the questionable glory of the pioneer past, the stories and counterstories, the contradictions inherent in ideals of independence and community, freedom and restriction—that contemporary western writers and revisionist historians are exploring today. Early in the novel, a bored high school teacher shakes her head at the worn-out themes her students have planned for their Pioneer Days parade float (based on Helena's Vigilante Days parade, a tradition that continues to this day). "Crossing the Plains, the Road Agents, the Vigilantes, the Gold Strike, the Shooting of Rattlesnake Jake. These Western children were more conscious of their pioneer past than New England children were of the Pilgrim Fathers."

Worse than a cliché is an obsession with the past. Harmless old Mr. Sewall in the Brandon Rapids hardware store devotes most of his time to keeping the records of the Montana Pioneer Society. The teenaged Pamela, typing his speeches for him, comes to know by heart his rolling sentences and his impossible and contradictory vision of the past. And while Mr. Sewall may be harmless, real danger lies in an obsession with the past that begins to distort the present. Pamela adores her father, an old-style Montana cattleman who seems to her a model of the strength and daring that settled the frontier. But when Charlie Lacey secretly borrows money against his cattle company and is ousted from his position as manager by his eastern partners, Pamela begins to see her father's risk-taking as foolish and his settle-with-a-handshake code as naïve.

Pamela tries to resolve her feelings about the West and its myths, represented by her father and his ranch hands, and the East and its pretensions, represented by her mother and by handsome Alan (nicknamed "the lady cowboy" by the ranch hands). Although she marries Alan, she can tolerate neither his condescension nor his finicky manners, so she comes home to convert the old home place into a successful dude ranch, rescuing her parents from penury but alienating her father and the ranch hands, who cannot abide the glossy surface of the new venture. Ruby, the tough ranch cook whose pithy advice has guided Pamela to womanhood, constantly points out that Pam is not a man and can never really head up a cattle outfit. The best Pamela can achieve—the dude operation—is a pandering of her heritage and a fraudulent reflection of the real thing.

I remember at this point becoming angry with Mildred Walker's plot line. What is Pam supposed to do? She had the guts to leave a stifling marriage, she has been supporting her parents as well as herself, and now she is punished for her courage by being made brittle and shallow. Where does Ruby get off, turning up her nose at the dude ranch and walking away from Pam? Where does Charlie Lacey get off, leaving Pam alone on the ranch so he can hang around the bar in the Western Hotel and drink and reminisce about the glory days? And Pam herself, agonizing over her failures as she tries to write her mother's obituary—why does Pam have to carry such a burden of guilt and loss?

It's true that the men in *The Curlew's Cry* tend to be disappointing. Pam sees that the autonomy and independence cherished by the mythmakers have been the ruin of her father when he comes up against a modern banking system, but when Wrenn, her high school sweetheart, says so out loud, she reacts defensively and breaks off her engagement to him. When Wrenn turns around and marries her best friend before she can forgive him, she disowns them both. She cannot accept imperfection; she knows that her father is flawed because he is a western man, true to the old code, but she believes her husband is flawed because he is not. Eventually she perceives even Wrenn as weak. After a series of disappointing suitors, she drops the most interesting, a labor organizer from Butte, when she sees him drunk. Divided as she is, Pam finally seems incapable of loving wholly.

But Mildred Walker never intended, in *The Curlew's Cry*, to portray the West as a man's brutal world in which women have no place, or to characterize men and women as separate beings in opposition to each other's worlds. "The concept of the Wilderness grew and grew for me as I wrote, and kept changing," she wrote, scolding me for taking a reductive view of her novel. "In *Curlew's Cry* it meant loneliness, being unloved, and finally loving no man."

Early in *The Curlew's Cry*, before her father's disgrace and bankruptcy, before her own loss of innocence and her quarrel with
Wrenn, Pam invites her friend Rose to spend a few days with
her at the ranch. Rose is startled by a curlew's cry. *What's that?*
she asks Pam.

> "Nothing but an old curlew bird," Pam said. "Curlews always
> make that sound. Ruby says it's the loneliest sound she knows."
> "It scared me," Rose said promptly.
> "Not when you know what it is. At least, I'm not afraid of
> it," Pamela answered.

Pamela, you'd better be afraid, I want to warn her as I reread
The Curlew's Cry today. You're about to find out the kind of a life
that is possible for a young woman who has come of age on the
last vestige of the frontier and who has absorbed its values as she
has lived up to its harsh physical demands. You're going to learn
that such a young woman can never accept the constraints of a
traditional female role, and yet she can never fully assume a male
role. You'll ask what space, then, you can claim, and what air is
yours to breathe? And what will you do for friends, companionship?

What hope, finally, for a single woman in her middle years?

In the conclusion of *The Curlew's Cry*, Mildred Walker does
allow Pamela Lacey to find her way back from the state of
anguish and isolation that apparently represents Walker's concept of wilderness. It is not quite a happy resolution. But it is,
perhaps, what Walker herself came to, with her children grown
and her beloved husband dead. Wistfulness was never her way,
nor could she retreat into an imagined past, any more than she
could have provided Pamela Lacey with Chip of the Flying U to
love, or one of Dorothy Johnson's outlaws to daydream about in
her dotage. Instead, she returned to New England and taught
for thirteen years at Wells College, from which she had graduated thirty years earlier. She wrote *If A Lion Could Talk*, and she
didn't move back to Montana until she was in her eighties, in ill
health, to live near her daughter, Ripley Schemm.

Walker's fiction, written outside the western myth, has come perilously close to being forgotten, and maybe that's the fate of mothers who write in isolation, without a tradition. But her novels are back in print at last, and while she may never have reconciled the dusty present with the western mythos, she opened a door between for me and so many others to follow her.

The Apostate in the Attic

I WAS TWELVE WHEN MY FATHER SOLD THE RANCH where he had been born and bought another, in the foothills of the Snowy Mountains, near Lewistown, Montana, so that my younger sisters and I could live at home when we were ready for high school. Other rural children might be boarded in town during their high school years, as he himself had been, or they and their mothers might live in rented houses during the week and come home on weekends. But my father would make any other sacrifice, even the sale of the home ranch, before he would let us go.

It was not a move any of us wanted to make, and even the weather seemed enraged by it. Blizzards swept across Montana the December that we moved. The pastures and roads were buried in snow, and the temperature dropped below zero and stayed there. When I cried, my mother told me that, if I felt bad, to think of how my grandmother must feel, who had lived so much of her life near Spring Creek, in the lap of the South Moccasin Mountains, and now would be moving with us.

My father and mother visited the new ranch once, before we made the move, and I went along. From Lewistown we turned south toward the Snowies, and soon the old truck was howling

Snowbound barn and spring house in the Snowy Mountains, 1952.

and grinding through the drifts on an unploughed road that wound deeper and deeper into pine-covered hills. The frozen stream at the bottom of the ravine was Casino Creek, which flowed down from Sawmill Gulch. We would be living only seven miles from town, I had been told, but the road seemed endless to me as it twisted and wound under the heavily snow-laden pines. Every new turn was unfamiliar, but finally the road broke out of deep timber and stopped at a pole gate. In the deep cleft between two forested ridges squatted a huge unpainted barn, some log sheds, and a square stone house with an unpainted lean-to sagging off its back door.

I got out of the warm truck and floundered through snow to a half-buried picket fence, where a gate opened between two young firs, and forced open the door to the lean-to. The dark chill smelled of mice and ancient smoke. I groped my way across the filthy, sloping board floor to an inner door that opened into a frigid kitchen.

Light fell through deep windows cut into the massive sandstone walls. My breath hung over the rusted linoleum in a frozen white puff. No fires had warmed this house for months, and those eighteen-inch sandstone walls had absorbed the frost to their core and radiated it back like a deep freeze. I only knew I had never been so cold. Hunched in my coat, my teeth chattering, I explored the downstairs rooms, the long kitchen that halved the house and, behind the kitchen, two smaller rooms connected by archways. Empty, echoing space. The deep windows, set two to a side, looked out on snow. I found myself listening, as though for footsteps, hostile whispers, warnings, but not a backward trace of occupancy could I find or hear.

Behind a dry sink in the kitchen I found a door to a stairway that led up to a hall with two bedrooms and space for what might have been a bathroom if the house had been plumbed. I looked out an upstairs window and saw our familiar truck parked by the picket fence. Whatever my mother and father were doing, they were nowhere to be seen. Opposite the house was an ancient log shed, sagging under a roof-load of snow, and a narrow gully choked with the cross-hatchings of bare chokecherry brush and hawthornes. Behind the gully rose a steep snowy hill, broken by more brush and sandstone boulders and outlined with pines so dark they looked black against the snow.

Shivering, I turned from the window and wandered into the larger of the two bedrooms. Stark, freezing, full of the white light of snow but otherwise empty except for a stack of old magazines next to a square hole cut in the floor. I looked through the hole and saw the bare floor of the room directly below.

I squatted down and examined the magazines. Fifteen or twenty back issues of *Ladies Home Journal. Good Housekeeping. Redbook.* I opened one and began to read about a world of dishwashers and matching living room suites. Tips on window treatments, easy-care hair styling, recipes for casseroles, and meal plans that contained the four basic food groups. By the time my mother found me and told me it was time to go home, my fingers were so numb with cold that I could barely turn pages.

The stone house had been built at the turn of the century by a homesteader who was also a stonemason. The old Ruckman house, some of the neighbors still called it. Over the years the blocks of stone had settled and cracked and been repaired with steadily decreasing levels of masonry skills. Flies laid their eggs in the cracks, to hatch and die in droves on the windowsills, and bats had filtered in and colonized the attic and were accidentally disturbed by my sisters and me the next spring, when we opened the trapdoor and ducked and screamed as we were swooped at. The old lean-to was so filthy and decrepit that my father bulldozed and burned it along with the rotting log sheds. He also hauled down the tottering old wind charger that once had supplied the Ruckmans with flickering electric lights but now threatened to crash down on the roof when the pines on the ridges wrung their boughs and roared in the wind like the surf.

And yet the stone house possessed a curious grace. Its firs and picket fence suggested the decorum of another time and place. Lilacs and willows grew around its scrap of lawn, and sandstone stepping stones led up to the seldom-used front door, where columbines bloomed every summer. The ceilings of the stone house were lofty, its walls had been finished with real plaster, its kitchen was wainscoted in oak that someone had lightened and brightened with several coats of thick tan paint. Of the most recent occupants, the young couple who had lived there a year and been so eager to sell out to my parents, the only trace I ever found was the stack of magazines.

More snow fell in these mountains than we had ever seen, and the narrow road down through the pines to town drifted shut for much of the winter. My younger sisters and I were excused from school when the bus didn't run, which it often didn't. But my father had sold the home ranch and bought this one so we could go to school, and go to school we would. He owned a war surplus jeep with a canvas top, and my sisters and I would pack ourselves in, shivering, in wool coats and scarves and overshoes, with wool pants under our obligatory school skirts. Into the clean white light we roared, past the barn and snowcapped corrals, through the pole gate, with my father peering to see the road through the palm-sized hole in the frost that he managed to keep scraped out of the windshield. His idea was to see how deep in snow he could force the jeep before it foundered. Kerwham! We'd hit the first drift, driving the jeep up to its fenders and sending an explosion of snow over the windshield and roof; and out would jump my father, shoveling and cursing. Sometimes it took us two hours to drive the seven miles down to Lewistown.

Then our neighbor down the gulch noticed what my father was doing. He hadn't been sending his daughters to school when the bus didn't run, but he rose to the challenge. The little Fullerton girls, bundled to their ears, were packed into the back of the jeep with my sisters and me, and Johnnie Fullerton climbed in beside my father with his shovel. Ker-wham! We'd hit a drift, the jeep would bury itself to the fenders in snow, and out would jump my father and Johnnie, shoveling and cursing. With the two of them, their cursing sounded almost a jubilant tone that rang with the scrapes of their shovels through the silent pines and the deep unmoving hills.

The secretary at school was always surprised to see me when I burst in, midmorning, with snow embedded in my clothes and my nose running from the sudden heat of the office. She would write me my slip, and I would duck into the girls' bathroom to haul off my overshoes and heavy wool pants, hang them with my coat and scarf in my locker, and run to whichever class I was on time for. Most of the time I would be the only girl from the country who had made it to school, and I would take my place in the cavernous old study hall with its creaking wood floors and its skylight in the rafters. Gradually my fingers and toes would thaw out, while the girls from town in their pearls and poodle cuts and billowing clothes whispered and passed notes to each

other, and the star basketball players, aloof as gods in their letter jackets, sat glazed-eyed with their feet on other people's
desks.

My father had started a dairy. He poured a concrete floor in the
old barn and installed milking stanchions, built a springhouse,
and bought big, lumbering cows with heavy udders, mottled
black-and-white Holsteins for the most part, with a few rangy
Brown Swiss and the occasional doe-eyed Guernsey. At least the
days of hand milking were long past. Three Surge milking
machines chugged away, powered by an electrical line he had
run in from the utility pole, but each milking still took two
hours. He was up at five in the morning, seven days a week,
winter and summer, to feed the cows and finish milking by
eight. At five in the afternoons he started all over again, feeding
and milking. In between he drove his daughters to school and
delivered milk to the creamery in ten-gallon cans, cleaned the
barns, attended to the unending ranch chores. In the summer
there was seeding and haying and harvesting.

To get everything done in twenty-four hours, we all helped.
My father washed udders and milked, but my grandmother laid
the grain in the stanchions and then worked in the springhouse,
washing equipment and straining the milk through filters and
pouring it into the cans, which she set to chill in a tank of
springwater. And either my mother or I carried every bucket of
milk the fifty yards down from the barn to the springhouse,
back and forth.

Milk-carrying was a monotonous, heavy, endless task. Out
of the cold and into the barn, where my glasses immediately
fogged up from the body heat of thirty milk cows munching the
feed in their stanchions and occasionally lifting their tails and
dropping a steaming green pile into the gutter. The reek of
manure blended with the smell of warm milk as my father,
crouched under a flank, wiped off an udder with a rag wrung
out in warm water and attached the suction cups to the teats

with a little hiss that turned into the rhythmic chug, chug of the milking machine. By that time, one of the other machines would be ready to be emptied. Full of milk, it would weigh nearly forty pounds. My father would unclip it from the surcingle that held it suspended under the cow's belly, take off the top, and step across the gutter where I waited for my buckets to be filled with the white, fragrant foam. Then he was off to attach the machine to another cow, and I was off with my buckets for another trip down to the springhouse. I was sulky about it, of course. I would rather have been doing anything else.

Frustrations, fatigue. The unrelenting routine took its toll. In the winter, the stars would be out long before we finished milking. And some of the cows were touchy about being milked, especially the Brown Swiss. With their heads locked in the stanchions, they couldn't get away, but they would wrench and struggle and try to kick. My father sometimes snapped a pair of metal kickers on their hocks, but more often he would loop a piece of half-inch rope around a cow's foot and lash her to one of the metal support posts that ran down the middle of the barn. While the cow rolled back her eyes, trying to see what he was doing, he'd make the perfunctory swipe with the rag wrung out in warm water and snap the suction cups on her teats.

Why he hadn't tied up that Brown Swiss on one particular night, I don't know. He stepped up to her with his pail of warm water and the milking machine, and she picked up that big cloven hind hoof and drove it right into his eye.

I was waiting with my buckets in that split second of absolute suspended time. The cow, the kick, my father's head reeling back. Then time resumed its normal speed, and my father reached for the old oak wheel-spoke that he kept handy, and he laid the wheel-spoke across the cow's flanks and back and sides in hard repeated blows, one two three four five six seven eight nine, and I lost count as the cow reared against her stanchion with her bell jangling, cringing as more blows thundered down on her, crashing when she lost her footing on the manure-smeared cement. Fifteen sixteen seventeen eighteen blows, and every cow in the barn was rearing back, thirty cows fighting their stanchions while their cowbells clanged.

He stopped when his arm wore out. The cow found her footing and stood trembling in every muscle while welts rose in a grid across her creamy brown hide. The confusion of cowbells up and down the barn gradually died. He turned, and he saw me, and I saw that half his face was imprinted by mud and manure and blood in the shape of that cloven hoof, while under that foul layer the flesh swelled and purpled around the single bloodshot eye.

During the spring and summer, the milk cows were turned out to pasture on the pine slopes, and my task was to ride out on horseback, morning and afternoon, and bring them in for milking. It might take me twenty minutes or two hours, depending on how deep into the underbrush they'd gone for grass or hiding from flies. I liked wrangling better than carrying milk. Mornings could be pleasant, with the alarm going off in the not quite daylight, my sisters still asleep in the opposite bed, my bare feet on the cool linoleum as I reached for my blue jeans. Silence from the other bedroom. My getting up for the morning wrangling meant that my father could get an extra hour or two of sleep.

Often I didn't bother with shoes, but slipped downstairs in the quiet of the stone house, pushing my hair back from my face and buttoning my shirt. Stars would be fading over the points of the firs by the picket fence, and I would close the gate behind me and pad the hundred yards to the barn, wincing if it was too early in the spring for my bare feet to have grown calluses. The little buckskin chore horse would be waiting for me in the corral.

I would slide a bridle over her head, mount her bareback, and ride up the hill to the night pasture with my fingers wound in her mane. At this hour, even the wind was usually still, even the owls gone home, and I would be listening for the faintest tinkle of cowbells. At least the night pasture was smaller than the day pasture, less choked with underbrush for cows to hide in, and sometimes I would find them right away, their big warm bodies looming up like mottled black-and-white boulders out of the grass where they had made their beds. As the days grew longer and the light broke earlier and earlier, they might already be grazing with their bells clanking, and I would count them—was I lucky, were they all here? Twenty-five, twenty-six, twenty-seven. Grace wasn't here, Verna wasn't here, Baby wasn't here —and Grace and Verna and Baby were the ramblers, likely to have climbed the ridge beyond this one, looking for grass, or maybe they were grazing on the slope in the opposite direction, and I would have to ride another loop, hunting and listening for the sound of their bells.

"How can you tell which is which?" asked one of my cousins from town. "They all look alike."

"No they don't," I said, although one of the first lessons I had learned in town school was that not everybody saw the world with the eyes I had been trained to see with, and I felt as though I was constantly shifting focus, from close to distant. "They all look different."

"They're all black and white."

"But they all look different."

Our old cow dog had made the move from the home ranch with us, but once he was living closer to town, he took to visiting other dogs and traveling in a pack. Can't have a dog that runs around the country, said my father, and had him put down. He bought a collie, but she was so sensitive that any noise or conflict sent her cowering under the lilac bush. Sometimes I could coax her along when I wrangled cows, but I didn't dare raise my voice or sic her on the cows, or she would be streaking through grass and briars for the safety of the lilac bush.

By June the heat and the deerflies were sometimes so oppressive that even on the morning wrangle I would ride for an hour or more and finally find the cows in little bunches of three or four, embedded in the underbrush in one of a dozen gullies with their bells absolutely still. They wouldn't want to move from the cool, even to be milked. I could yell, swear—there went the collie, a shuddering wreck running for her lilac bush— I could throw stones that crashed down through the hawthorne leaves over their heads, and still the cows wouldn't move. Nothing for it but to duck my head and ride down one of the little deer trails into the gully with pine boughs lashing at me and the horse and hawthornes swatting me in the face. Prod one cow to her feet, prod another, try to get everybody moving. Sometimes the brush was so dense that I dismounted and crawled through it, and then I was thankful for the little buck-skin chore horse, who never fought the thorns or reared up and tried to see over them, but ducked her head and followed me at the end of the bridle reins I had slung over my shoulder.

When school started in the fall, I was embarrassed by the cross-hatched scratches and scars on my arms and legs, left by pine stubs and thorns. "Wear my leather chaps," my father advised me, "and a Levi jacket." He made a good story about the time when, at the height of deerfly season, he wondered why I was taking so long with the cows, went looking for me, and met me crawling out of a patch of thornbrush on my hands and knees, with Buck the chore horse right behind me.

I dreaded having my glasses knocked off my face by some lashing branch, and one morning it happened. I felt them go, and I sat petrified on my horse for a moment, looking at a world that had suddenly turned to blurred greens and blues where once had been pine needles and gnarled boughs, twigs and scal-loped hawthorne leaves, soft fringes of cinquefoil and grass and low-growing bunches of Oregon grape. Oh god. What was I going to do. How far had they flown. What if Buck moved a hoof, one more step, and crunched my glasses. I slid off her back, hoping I wouldn't be on top of my glasses, and squatted down with my nose a few inches from mountain soil.

I knew that the glasses would be hard to spot, being transparent, and I groped this way and that, crying. At close focus, the pine needles rematerialized in a mat of brown compost and individual spears of grass poking up through darker loam where ants scurried through decaying leaves and up my ankles on who knew what frantic errands of their own. Gasping, praying that Buck wouldn't shift a hoof, I felt this way and that, and at last my hand bumped into my glasses, caught on a clump of buckbrush about a foot off the ground. I stuck them back on my face and saw the world take shape again, trails and branches, boulders and grass and sky.

No one should ever try to hurry a milk cow, and not just because the milk cow doesn't want to, but because hurrying will reduce her milk flow. Being startled or frightened will also reduce a cow's milk flow, not just for one milking, but gradually over a whole season, even over her milking lifetime. For the sake of their milk production, cows should lead calm lives, eating and loafing and taking all the time in the world to walk from pasture to stanchion and back again. Milk cows should not be driven frantic by buzzing swarms of deerflies and then chased from the sanctuary of the deep brush by shouts and stones from an angry girl who will prod or lash them into a trot or even a gallop if she can just get them headed for the barn. Wild-eyed, bells a-jangle, crashing against each other into the corral, their great udders swinging back and forth, teats leaking milk—not the way to treat milk cows at all.

When the cow kicked my father in the eye, he must have seen, with the revolving stars behind his eyelids, the frustration of the past years. The sacrifice of the home ranch, the unfamiliar mountain pastures. The reeking foot rot that had infested his milk cows, swelling their poor cloven hooves until they split, requiring an expensive series of penicillin shots for a cure. The premature calves, born dying or dead because the cows had been feeding on pine needles. Their reduced milk production. A reduction in the price of butterfat. The dairy inspectors who found floating bits of barnyard contamination in the milk. The debts.

Other forces that he couldn't have foreseen. He knew that times were tough, that other dairymen were selling out or retiring, but he didn't know that economic pressures were going to make a small, family-run dairy as obsolete as the horse-drawn rakes and seeders he had inherited from his father. The three Lewistown creameries that bought raw Grade A milk from local dairies would close their doors in a few years. The dozen or so small dairies clustered within ten miles of town would dwindle, finally disappear. And just as supermarkets replaced the corner groceries, butter was replaced by margarine and locally bottled milk by mass-produced milk shipped in plastic jugs from centralized dairies as far away as western Washington State.

Teresa Jordan's memoir of coming of age on a Wyoming ranch, *Riding the White Horse Home*, is one of the most beautiful books I know. How ironic, Teresa once pointed out to me, that she, whose parents always expected her to leave the ranch, who in fact sent her to boarding school and eventually to Yale University, has spent the rest of her life trying to return; while I, who was expected never to leave the ranch, have spent the rest of my life trying to get away. Looking for the reasons why this is true, I come back to the stone house.

Plastered walls contain a certain fragrance, a stored coolness that overlies ancient lath and horsehair. Painted over or wallpapered, they never feel quite like modern drywall. Sawed timbers shift, open cracks in the walls, keep the family secrets but let in the flies and the bats. My mother fought the flies and the mice, and she fumigated the bedsprings with kerosene to get rid of the bedbugs. Summer and winter, she worked however many hours it took to wash every thread of clothes we wore in a wringer washer, hang them out on a line to bake or freeze dry, and carry them in by armloads to sprinkle and iron. She was thankful to have a refrigerator, she did without running water and drains, she helped in the dairy, she cooked every bite we ate, three meals a day, 365 days a year, and she washed up in a dishpan she had to fill from a bucket and empty in the yard. And all this with my youngest sister tugging at her skirt and pleading for the attention that my mother had no time to give her.

Not that, as a teenager, I gave any thought to my mother's workload.

"Mary, play with this kid! Read to her! Anything! At least long enough for me to get these dishes washed!"

"Why do I have to?" I whined. I had an hour before it would be time to wrangle milk cows, and I wanted to spend it reading to myself.

I looked for places to hide. Some of the best were in my head. Riding after the cows in the afternoons, I would come upon the hollows crushed down by deer where they had bedded in the grass, and I would imagine living inside that warmth of hide and fur. Nibbling on browse, needing nothing else, no fires, blankets, baggage. But I couldn't see through the eyes of a doe for very long, couldn't will myself into the absolute still, the lovely long ears and slope of neck, the slender legs—and I was a realist ranch kid, after all, I knew what happened to deer. Once, searching for milk cows, I had ridden along the fence between our gulch and the next and found the dried hide and bones of a doe that hadn't quite cleared the barbed wires, caught her hindquarters on a strand, and hung there, struggling, until she weakened and starved.

No. I would never leave my mind behind. Better to build a shelter for it and myself, out of deadfall in the deepest leaves, or overhead in the pine boughs, with needles for bed and blanket and a fire to read by—but that plan woke up the realist in a hurry. *Light a fire in the pines? What are you thinking about? Do you realize how dry that timber is? What are you trying to do, set the whole gulch on fire?*

Looking for privacy in the early years of the century, when

the stone house was built, would have seemed perverse at a time when no magic power lines or telephone lines connected the mountain homesteads with town and its services. The big kitchen in the stone house would have been the gathering place by kerosene lamplight, the whole family sitting in a circle, in a bulwark against the dark. Some would be knitting or darning, some would be reading with the pages tilted toward the lamp, some would be recounting the small events of the day or the year, telling the same stories over and over again. When the wicks were snuffed out and the family gone to bed, the pines drawn closer to the clearing until their serrated tips looked like teeth biting into the clouds that blew past the moon, then the comfort of those rooms with their two or three double beds and the quietly breathing humps of brothers or sisters or snoring grandparents would have lulled the children to sleep.

And yet, and yet. Did some daughter of that family slide quietly out of her body and float to the ceiling in the transparent globe of her mind? Did she look back at her sleeping kinsfolk with her divided vision?

My parents slept in the upstairs room with the square hole in the floor that let heat rise from the stove downstairs. My sisters and I slept in the other room, and my grandmother had a bed in the hall. With no plumbing, a nighttime urge meant either a cold walk under the stars to the outhouse or else the sneak through the hall to the chamber pot behind the curtain in the room which might have been meant for a bathroom but which my mother had filled with boxes of odds and ends that took on ominous shapes in the dark. No sound was a secret, not the snores and twitches, not the creaks and heavy breathing from the bedroom next door, not the stealthy pad of footsteps in the hall or the fizz of a hot stream being released into the pot. Trying not to listen made every fart and groan more intense.

I had begun to mature after the move to the stone house, and my mother had provided me with an elastic belt and safety pins and bulky pads, which I tried to change without being watched by curious little sisters. I cringed at the way my shirts rubbed against my sore nipples, hated the way my breasts bounced and ached when I rode horseback. A woman's body was nothing I had ever wanted, and nothing my mother had ever wanted for me, either, I could tell by her new watchfulness, her face halfway between anger and derision.

"What do you want to take a bath so often for?" everybody asked me. "What have you been working so hard at, that you think you're dirty?"

The physical education teacher at school had lectured all the girls on personal hygiene. The daily bath, the shaved legs and armpits, the antiperspirant. Envying the girls from town for the way they seemed to flaunt their hips and breasts and yet disengage themselves from bodily nastiness, I dragged out the galvanized tub every night, set it up in the kitchen, and filled it with hot water from a bucket, sat in soap scum with my knees under my chin, and worried about my flaws. Picked at the beaded rows of scabs along the fresh thorn scratches, licked the white lines of old scars and wondered if they would ever fade. Were my feet too big? I stuck a leg out of the tub, tried the rotating exercise that some book in the home economics room at school said would make my ankles more slender.

Everyone would have gone to bed except my father, who sat reading at the kitchen table and trying not to look at me. When had my father ever been embarrassed by my naked body? What had happened, since the move to the stone house, to change us all? I wished I knew a way, like putting my glasses back on, that would bring us all back into a familiar focus.

In my search for privacy, I tried the attic. It must have been deep summer, because I remember the stale heat in my face when I lifted the trapdoor, not for the first time, of course, but the other times I had been chased off by the bats. But now the bats were gone, killed off, perhaps, by the D-Con my mother had put down to poison the mice. I hoisted myself through the square hole in the ceiling and found myself in a closed space of rafters and shadows, illuminated by a single dirty window.

I couldn't take a step without crunching on the mouse droppings—or bat droppings—that littered the floorboards. And what was there to see? Through the little dormer window, an expanse of shingled roof and the tops of the firs, oddly foreshortened when seen from above. Behind me on a nail hung the fiddle that had been my grandfather's, its bow and strings lost long ago, its soundboard chewed by mice.

If my grandfather's fiddle had been stored there, the attic must also have held other family odds and ends, stowed away after the move from the home place. And yet I remember seeing none of these things. No boxes of canning jars, no boxes of old clothing or odd dishes—what else would there have been? Sometimes it seems to me that there was a trunk—but maybe that is because, along with an old fiddle, every attic is expected to hold a trunk, and memory is only too likely to retain its expectations.

What one corner of the attic held—and this I am certain of, because I possess them today—were three very old books, nibbled at their corners and swollen as if from moisture that had long dried. Curious, with no premonition, I lifted them out of the dust and flyspecks and examined them. After all, I was always looking for something to read. The first book was red, or had once been red. Stamped in gold on its cover was *Junior Latin Reader: Sanford and Scott.* Also in gold on the cover was an emblem like a torch, stamped mysteriously with the initials SPQR. On its endpapers was a map, labeled Imperium Romanum, and a penciled price, 1⁵⁰. I turned another page and found, also written in pencil, notes on the use of the dative case with verbs meaning to favor, help, please, trust, believe, persuade, command, obey, serve, resist, envy, threaten, pardon & spare.

Latin was still taught at that time in my high school, but usually not to girls from the country, who were thought to have more practical aims than a filigreed, college-bound diploma. As I held that book in my hands, I felt as though I were opening another window, too dirty to see through clearly, but offering a limitless expanse.

The second book was brown, stamped in black with *Arnold's Latin Prose Composition* and a border of acanthus leaves. Its price had been 1⁸⁰, and it held another clue—"Fran" Ruckman, written in spidery ink. So! A daughter of this very house. (Or could "Fran" have been a son? A daughter, I decided, emphatically.)

The third book was in the worst condition, its maroon cover mottled pink with waterspots. From the label inside, it had once been the property of the University of Montana library. Its pages were stained and speckled, but it was the first of these books that I could read. Its title was *Julian: Philosopher and Emperor: and the Last Struggle of Paganism against Christianity,* by Alice Gardner, Lecturer and Associate of Newnham College, Cambridge, Author of "Synesius of Cyrene," published in 1906.

Below me in the hall, my sisters had set up a dollhouse and were having a fight between the dolls. Their quarreling voices rose to the attic, but I deliberately shut my ears. Squatting in the dust, in the fecal heat under the eaves, by gold light sifted through an encrusted window, I began to read about an apostate emperor who had been raised a Christian but, loving classical letters and learning, had ascended to the throne of the Holy Roman Empire in A.D. 355, turned his back on the cross, and set the pagan gods back in their pantheon. It was the first time I had ever come across the word *apostate*.

"Fran Ruckman," said my Latin teacher, thoughtfully, at the University of Montana a few years later. "She must have been a student of mine."

I have never heard Fran Ruckman's name spoken since then, although I still possess her books. Whether, from the ragbag of her adolescence, out of shadowy scraps of motives and urges, conscious choices and half-conscious responses, Fran Ruckman pieced together the reasons why she attended the University of Montana in the early years of the twentieth century, whether she supposed that she was running away from hard work and responsibilities, or whether she thought she was running after her mind and taking her body with her, I have no way of knowing. Did Fran Ruckman wear glasses? When she bought a book written in 1906 by a woman scholar, did she think of herself as an apostate? Did her dreams drift as far and remote as the spires of Newnham College, Cambridge?

Did Fran Ruckman ever learn anything about double vision, about the shapes of individual blades of grass an inch from her nose, and how she lost sight of those shapes when she put her glasses back on to look at the horizon? Did she imagine that she had to choose between a close focus and the longer view?

Did she intend never to come home again, and if so, how did her old Latin textbooks happen to be stored for years in the attic of the old Ruckman house? After wandering the far corridors of sleepless nights, did she find herself again and again in that attic, under that encrusted window in the odor of bats and mice? Sifting dust, endlessly, compulsively, trying to understand.

The Judith

A S ALWAYS, I RETURN TO RIVERS AND ESPECIALLY TO the Judith, which is an obscure blue stream that begins in the Little Belt Mountains in central Montana and winds for only about sixty miles before it flows into the Missouri at a place called the Judith Landing. Its beautiful name is a mistake. In 1805 Captain William Clark, exploring much farther up that blue current than did his companion, Captain Meriwether Lewis, named it for a girl back in Fincastle, Virginia, whose name really was Julia. What a romantic story, I remember thinking, when, as a child, I was told how Clark had named our Judith River for his sweetheart and Lewis had named the Marias River, up north, for his. Yes, and Clark eventually went home and married his Julia, while Lewis returned, not to the shadowy Maria, but to a tortured and solitary death, murder or suicide, no one is sure which.

"We . . . came to a handsome river which discharges on the south, and which we ascended to the distance of a mile and a half," Lewis wrote on May 29, 1805. "Its entrance is 100 yards wide from one bank to the other. . . . The water is clearer than any which we have yet seen; and the low grounds, as far as we could discern are wider and more woody than those of the

Missouri. Along its banks we observed some box-elder inter-
mixed with cottonwood and willow, the undergrowth consisting
of rosebushes, honeysuckles, and a little red-willow."

The clear water and the willows that Lewis described were
virtually unchanged when I last rode horseback along the same
stretch of the Judith that he and Clark explored. That horseback
ride was in the 1970s, and I was a different woman then. I had
recently been divorced, and my children—my two older children, my first family; my second family and subsequent life as
yet undreamed of—were spending summers with my parents on
the ranch in the Snowy Mountains, in Fergus County. I was working at Northern Montana College in Havre, on the Highline, and
I used to drive down to visit my children, dressed in my fashionable thigh-high skirts and ankle-length linen duster and driving
my 1972 MG Midget at a high rate of speed over the cutoff road
through the Fort Belknap reservation. Once or twice during those
years the Fort Belknap tribal police pulled me over for going
eighty miles an hour across darkened prairie at three in the morning. How I must have looked in the eyes of the tribal cop who had
to bend nearly double to see into the rolled-down window of my
MG, I can only imagine now, with embarrassment.

On this particular occasion, the 4-H club that my children
belonged to was sponsoring a trail ride along the lower Judith
River. My father lent me a horse and saddle, and I brought my
old boots and Levis and joined fifty other riders of all ages for a
slow July day of heat and horseflies, the glitter of river water over
gravel bars, and the welcome shade of the willows. In a splash-
ing line, to the grace notes of children's voices, we must have
forded the Judith fifteen or sixteen times as it looped and dou-
bled through alfalfa fields and bottomland pastures just out of
sight behind giant cottonwoods seeded from trees seeded from
the ones Lewis and Clark saw. The bighorn sheep, the *argali* that
the two captains noted in their journals, were long gone, but we
spooked deer out of their leafy daylight beds and annoyed a
heron into long-legged flight.

At the Judith Landing, at midday, we were met by a stock truck, bringing our lunches. I dismounted, stiffly enough, from the gentle white mare I was riding, and was asked, did I want a ride home in the truck? No, I said. I was ashamed, offended even, to be mistaken for the woman I pretended to be, the girl who wore contact lenses and teased her hair into a bubble, who had a Ph.D. in English literature and a handful of published short stories. Maybe my father had time, nowadays, to ride for pleasure with his grandchildren, but when I had been my children's age, riding had been work, and I had done my share. Pleasure riding indeed! I could still sit a horse as long as anyone could. And I did, all the way back to the ranch where we had started, refording the river another fifteen or sixteen times as shadows stretched down from the bluffs, the small gnats rose above the water, and the air cooled.

During the afternoon, the woman who owned the land rode up beside me and pointed out a rotting post or two in a clump of burdock growing out of the bare slope above the willows.

"That was a homestead cabin," she said. "I can remember, in the 1930s, when the woman who filed on the claim still lived there by herself. The story was that she had been a concert pianist in New York. She had a portable phonograph, and records that she played in the evening."

No ghostly piano recording followed us in the dark when we rode into the yard lights at the ranch. I was riding beside the legendary Julia Jackson Snyder, who, with my father, had been a charter member of the first 4-H club in Fergus County, back in the 1920s, and now, in her late seventies, was still training her own horses and competing in hundred-mile endurance rides. I think Julia might have been keeping a concerned eye on me. But I unsaddled the white mare myself, and climbed the porch steps to the ranch house for coffee and barbeque with everyone else. At eleven o'clock that night, with the three-hour drive to Havre ahead of me, I was so tired that I had to lift one of my legs with my hands, and then the other leg, into the MG.

A much older name for the Judith is the Yellow River. In his novel *Fools Crow*, James Welch describes a Blackfeet war party riding south along the Yellow River into Crow territory to raid their horses. In an age when space satellites travel over Montana, it takes an act of will to imagine what the Blackfeet saw. And yet the golden willows and ripe chokecherries, the wild roses and the scent of mint—*quicksmell*—were as familiar to the Blackfeet as the soft crunch of unshod hooves on gravel, as sweat and river water streaming down flanks. As familiar as the drift of fluff from the cottonwoods into the current was to me then, and is now. The world as it was and is.

My childhood world was defined by the Judith, which curved in a deep blue bend around the sagebrush promontory where a log house and corrals had been built by one of the early white settlers in Fergus County. The ranch was still known as the Barney place when, shortly after their marriage, my mother and father moved in with a few sticks of furniture and a battered Ford truck, twenty horses, and a hundred head of white-faced cattle whose bloodlines my father was trying to improve with a couple of registered Hereford bulls. My parents were Montana born, and pleasure was not something that they expected to experience. They had seen their own homesteading parents struggle through the terrible twenties, when drought winds blew and crops failed and all the tailors and shopkeepers and doctors and teachers and concert pianists who had come to Montana to make a new life on the land drifted away with the dust. My parents' years were the dirty thirties, which they survived with hard work and austerity. My father put up hay with teams of horses. My mother raised a garden with alkali water she pumped from a well. Kerosene for the lamps, gas for the truck, and a few shells for the rifle were all they paid hard money for.

Mary Clearman Blew, 1940. I'm about a year old, riding Pardner. You can see my dad behind the horse, and the log home in the background.

When I was born, Aunt Rebie warned my mother, "You'll never raise that child, living down there so close to the river! She'll drown!"

"Oh, she'll learn to stay away from the river," said my mother. At least, that was how she told the story: Aunt Rebie's warning and her own grim certainty that I would learn my limitations, that, on pain of the business end of a belt wrapped around my legs, I would never want to follow that endless blue current out of sight.

An early memory. A car pulls up to the wire fence, then someone knocks at the door of the log house. My mother goes to answer. I hide behind her, overwhelmed by the novelty of a strange face, the presence of a strange young man. He wears— or is this a dream of mine?—a white shirt and blue pants. Another young man waits in the car. On top of the car—how can I, who have never seen a boat, know what they have hauled up to our house? Why do I remember it as a red rowboat?

But a boat it was, and I know now, from being told the story, that the young men planned to float in that boat, all the way down the Judith to the Missouri. They had come that day to ask my mother's permission to leave their car below the barn and launch their boat at the cattle crossing.

"Let's us walk down to the river and watch them start out," says my mother.

To be invited, by my mother, to approach the river! My heart pounds, my head is so light that I hold her hand as we pick our way through the sagebrush and sunbleached bunch-grass to the promontory, where we watch the young men lift down their boat and set it into the water. They strip off their shirts, they load their gear. If my hand weren't being held so tight, I would run and be loaded in that boat, too. And then they are afloat, bobbing on the blue current, rapidly merging into the white glare of the sun that fills my eyes with spinning spots. When I look again, the river is empty.

Days or weeks later, my mother says, "Do you remember those boys with their boat? They never made it to the Missouri. They got caught in an undercurrent and almost drowned. Hah! They should never have tried such a fool stunt. That river is more dangerous than people think."

Somehow the boys were pulled out of the Judith, badly sun-burned, bones broken, their boat lost—I don't know how I know these details. And yet they lived. One of them was Jack Norman, of Havre. I knew him years later, but I never asked him about his boat ride.

Another early memory. A scene, hardly more than an instant in a child's inarticulated dark consciousness. My father lies on the promontory, sighting his rifle at the river. Yards below him, at the base of the shale cutbank, the current has slowed and deepened into a dark green hole. A glimpse of underwater silver, my father fires his rifle, and the green surface breaks and thrashes to a white foam. For a moment the crack of the shot reverberates from the rimrocks and jack pine on the far side of the Judith, then fades. My father is shooting carp.

Death and the Judith. THE MOST ATROCIOUS CRIME EVER COMMITTED IN MONTANA, screams an 1889 headline of the *Fergus County Argus*.

> Last Saturday evening one of the cowboys on the Moccasin roundup rode into town and announced that the body of a woman had been found in the Judith river near what is known as Sample's crossing, about twenty-five miles below Lewistown. . . . The bodies of two men, two women and a child were taken from the river Tuesday afternoon and thoroughly examined by the coroner. All came to their deaths by violence. The two women were shot. . . . one man was shot through the heart and the other was killed by having his head crushed with a dull instrument; while the child, a girl of about six years, showed no marks of violence and it is presumed she was strangled to death. All the bodies were well, if not richly dressed, and considerable jewelry, such as finger and ear rings, breast and scarf pins, were found on their persons.

They had been the Kurtz and Briggs families, and they had driven up from Helena in their fine wagon and horses to look for ranchland in central Montana. They had been camped near Castle Butte, in the Snowies, when a James Wilber, of Great Falls, came upon them. Two years earlier, Wilber had been tried and acquitted in Wyoming in the killing of a herder. Now he shot the adults and strangled—or perhaps drowned—the little girl and loaded the bodies in their own wagon. His motive is obscure. Robbery, perhaps—he kept the fine horses and the wagon, but he left the jewelry on the bodies, which he hauled down to the Judith and buried in a gravel bar, about a mile upstream from the log house of my childhood.

Or perhaps Wilber's reasons were more twisted. "[He] was well known around Great Falls for his practical jokes of pointing loaded guns at people. More often than not, the punch lines of Wilber's jokes were delivered with a firm squeeze of the trigger," the *Lewistown Daily News* reported in 1958 when, in a macabre spirit of civic competition with Nebraska and the killing spree of Charles Starkweather, it resurrected Wilber's story under the headline "'starkweather type' murderer killed five: central montana had multiple slayer."

Wilber's story was one of those communal narratives in which everyone in sparsely settled Fergus County had a part to tell. In 1958 a clerk of the court remembered how his father, mistaking the hastily gathered posse for horse thieves, almost shot the sheriff. My grandmother remembered her mother-in-law's story, how Wilber had stopped by her homestead cabin and asked, without getting down from his wagon, the way to the river. Digging through the old records, I discovered that my great-grandfather, Abraham Hogeland, had been foreman of the coroner's jury that examined the bodies as they were exhumed from the gravel bar. And a neighbor's wife sent her children to gather wildflowers and gave her linen bedsheets for shrouds for the strangers.

The sheriff and his posse found Wilber a few days later, still with the horses and wagon, peeling potatoes to cook over his campfire. They took him at gunpoint to jail in Great Falls, where he remarked to another prisoner, "They couldn't convict me of killing the herd boy, but they will have no trouble in convicting me now." That night he hanged himself in his cell. He was buried in a potter's field in Great Falls. A few weeks later the earth of his grave was found disturbed, the grave empty. "Whatever has been the fate of Wilber's body, none regret that it will no longer desecrate the cemetery where the ashes of the good and virtuous should be free from such contamination," concluded the *Fergus County Argus* at the time.

Death and the river. Contrary to the *Fergus County Argus*, the most atrocious crime in Montana had already been committed, back in 1870, when Major Eugene M. Baker and the Second

Cavalry attacked a sleeping Blackfeet village on the Marias River and killed 173 Indians, including 53 women and children. Baker had been trailing killers who had already fled to Canada. He attacked the wrong village by mistake. When he discovered that some of the surviving Blackfeet children had been exposed to smallpox, he left them to die in the snow.

On the prairie slopes above the Judith River, in midsummer, there thrives a wildflower, *Castilleja linariaefolia*, which we call Indian paintbrush, so prolific that the ranch children in the summer of 1889 might have gathered armloads for the graves of the murdered strangers. Its stems are grayish yellow, its leaves fringed and narrow and tipped in vermillion, as though dipped in blood.

In a book called *Old Man's Garden*, a long out-of-print study of the flowers and grasses of the Montana and western Canadian prairies, Annora Brown explains the color of the paintbrush by telling a story about an Indian girl who fell in love with a wounded prisoner and ran away with him. I don't know where Annora Brown got the story, or whether it is authentic. But I hear it much differently than the girl with the short skirts and the bubble hair would have heard it in 1972.

> She longed for just one glimpse of her people and their camp. At last she could bear it no longer but made her way back to the hill above her home. Hidden in the bushes, she heard passing riders discussing her and telling of the punishment that was her due for her traitorous action. Knowing she could never make her presence known to her people she decided to take back with her a drawing of her home. Cutting a gash in her foot, she dipped a twig in the blood and drew, on a piece of bark, a picture of the camp in the valley before her. Then, throwing the twig to the ground, she made her way back to her adopted home. Where the twig fell there grew up a little plant with a brush-like end, dyed with the blood which the girl had used for paint.

They say that water purifies itself, every hundred yards or so, when it ripples over gravel in direct sunlight, and they also say that those cleansed droplets, sparkling on their incessant way, have been flowing from the beginning of time, from the steam of ancient fires and melted ice, from the clouds and mists, from the wells and springs of the earth. It is also said that time heals all wounds, and I have often wondered whether this can be true; whether, like the water, the drops of blood are reabsorbed, whether the cries eventually are soothed, whether forgiveness finally finds us all.

The Exhausted West

THE LOCAL LEGEND, WHEN I WAS GROWING UP IN Fergus County, was that the county seat, Lewistown, was the exact geographical center of Montana. In fact, the story went, the *exact* center of Montana was the drainpipe of the kitchen sink in a certain old brick mansion on upper Main Street. High school teachers tried to explain to us that a land surveyor could never be so accurate as to pick out a single town, let alone the drainpipe of a kitchen sink, as the *exact* center of an irregularly shaped state, but we third- and fourth-generation Montana kids knew better.

In 1986 that old brick house with its kitchen sink and its drainpipe was torn down and replaced by a McDonald's, but I can still stand at the top of Main Street Hill and see, past the golden arches, what I once thought was permanent and enduring: the green watered lawns and weeping willows around the Fergus County courthouse, the old Carnegie Library, built from dressed sandstone, with its slitted windows and crumbling stone steps, and, farther down the hill, the tops of cottonwoods shading the cattywampus streets. In the distance lies prairie and the blue shoulders of the Judith Mountains. On a clear day I can even see the outline of the Bear's Paw Mountains, faint as a cloud on the Montana Highline along the Canadian border, nearly two hundred miles away.

On slow summer days it is almost possible to believe that Lewistown has segued into a perpetual D.C. al fine. Like the old library, its ninety-year-old hotels and banks and store buildings were built from dressed sandstone by Croatian stonemasons around the turn of the century, or else from locally fired dark red bricks to last another century. The Bon Ton on Main Street still spreads its striped awning, still offers "cards for all occasions, fountain service, books and magazines—your coffee-break headquarters," with heavy tumblers upside down on a towel behind the soda fountain, freshly sliced lemons, and ice in a bin. Down the street, the white marble façade of the Montana Buildings, all six stories of it, gleams in dusty afternoon sunlight. Then the jangle of bars, the neon cowboy hats and cocktail glasses, the Moose Lodge and the Coast to Coast store. Where the historic T. C. Powers Mercantile used to display dry goods and quality footwear in a hush of decorum behind plate-glass doors, an Anthony's store now fills its windows with marked-down western wear and props its doors open to the sidewalk to send odors of linoleum and special-shipment sales goods into slow traffic.

Central Montana is a beautiful place. Fresh springwater, thousands of gallons a minute of the purest water in the world, gushes out of its foothills and flows through Lewistown on its way to the Judith River. Antelope drift through the fabulous grasslands, and white-tailed deer browse among the chokecherries and aspens at the bottoms of coulees. The subtle colors of wildflowers—Indian paintbrush and wild sweetpeas and prairie flax—burnish the sidehills. The coyotes have come back, after years of being systematically poisoned or hunted from airplanes, and at night their insubstantial yammer haunts the ridges. Cougars have been seen in the foothills of the mountains that ring the town. There is talk of wolves. And the price of land has recently veered toward the stars as an overflow of wealthy urban fugitives has sought an unspoiled alternative to Aspen or Sun Valley or Whitefish.

My great-grandfather, a land surveyor working for the Northern Pacific Railroad, came to Montana when it was still a territory, in 1882. He wrote home about the wonderful natural resources of the Judith Basin, its water and timber and deep grass, and he left the railroad and filed on a homestead to raise sheep and eventually survey much of Fergus County for the homestead land rush of 1910–1914. He believed—I think he would never have questioned—that he was bringing pastures and gardens to fruition in an empty landscape. That his purpose was to transform place into property. That, lovely as he found the pristine landscape, the choice between preserving it and fencing and plowing it was no choice at all.

I listened to the family stories as I grew up, but eventually I discovered the frontier myth spinners and learned from novels like A. B. Guthrie, Jr.'s *The Big Sky* still another way to understand the place where I was growing up. The mountain men in *The Big Sky* found in the Montana wilderness a paradise of wildlife and spectacular, unexplored scenery; the civic institutions that my great-grandfather had worked so hard to establish were the very constraints that Boone Caudill and Jim Deakins tried to escape when they made for the heart of the Blackfeet territory in the Tetons. And while my great-grandfather despised Indians all his life for what he saw as laziness and backwardness, the Indians in *The Big Sky* led idyllic lives in an untarnished landscape until they were corrupted by contact with the whites. It seemed to me that Guthrie had turned the whole pioneer narrative upside down. Men and women like my great-grandparents hadn't brought progress to the West. No indeed, they had brought disease, crime, poverty, erosion, prejudice, greed— because each man kills the thing he loves most. The mountain men had killed the beaver and opened trails for the explorers and surveyors, who were followed by the cattlemen and then by the miners and loggers and homesteaders, and each in turn had whittled and dug and burned and devastated what had been one of the most beautiful places on earth.

Mary's grandfather with horses and hay sled, 1910.

In spite of my reading—perhaps because of it—I thought that my life as a skim-milk Montana ranch kid was anything but colorful. Somewhere might exist the West I was reading about in the novels of Zane Grey, I thought. Texas, possibly, or Arizona. Or perhaps everything exciting had happened in the past. Nobody I knew in Fergus County was shooting his way out of bars or riding with the Hash Knife Outfit or being pursued through the purple sage by hostile Mormons. My family and all our neighbors lived in a perfectly ordinary way, working sixteen hours a day with teams of horses to mow and buckrake and stack their hay, and coming back tired to the house at night for a supper cooked on a wood stove, and later telling stories around the kitchen table or reading Zane Grey or Norman O. Fox by the light of kerosene.

I did know one family of Mormons. They had bought a ranch on the bench above ours and were trying to make a living raising potatoes. Their children, Dixie and Bradley, went to the one-room district school with my sister and me. The most exciting thing any of those Mormons ever did was get into a fistfight with the big boss of the Deerfield Hutterite colony over irriga-

Threshing wheat in Fergus County, 1910.

tion rights. I never saw the fight, of course, but I heard the men telling about it. I suppose they embroidered it—how old Eli Stahl, the Hutterite, was big and fat and bearded and thought he could bluff little Jack Grover, but what Eli didn't know was that Jack was an amateur featherweight boxing champion—*By God, Jack hit that fat bastard so hard that he fell right into his own irrigation ditch!*

It would be years before that episode would strike me as *story*, and western story at that.

I couldn't have known that my ordinary world had for years been shaped and altered by the expectations and desires of the "outside," that for nearly two centuries painters and writers from "civilization" had been venturing west and bringing back word of strange animals, exotic landscapes, and colorful customs. The last thing I could have imagined was that my family and I might be "local color." And I remember how surprised I was in 1975, when I got a note from the editor of a literary journal who had rejected a short story I had submitted to him. "But, God," he added, "how I envy you, living out there in that beautiful country."

Nor could I have imagined living in a museum. Just before I left Montana in 1987, I took my aunt to visit a homestead museum on the Montana Highline, where I had been living. My aunt was born in 1910 and had grown up on a homestead herself. She looked at the replica shack with its washtub and wood stove and lanterns and remarked, "I just hate it when I see things on display that I, personally, have *used*."

In his essay "On Going Back to Sawtooth Valley," the Idaho writer John Rember reflects on his childhood in the (relatively) pristine Sawtooth and how, just after World War II, he and his family were thrilled when they finally were hooked up with electrical power service. Returning as an adult to live and write in the Sawtooth, Rember is struck by the changes in his remote and sheltered valley, where rivers teem with fish-hatchery salmon and trout, and federal legislation protects the scenery:

> There has been talk of burying the main power lines that run along the highway in order to enhance the pastoral values of the valley yet another degree. The power company doesn't think it's practical. The cold of the winters here would make it impossible to dig down to a frost-damaged line. But I hope they figure out a way to get around that problem, because along with the Forest Service, I think it would look better. The lines are a visible reminder of our intimate connection to the world that lies outside the valley walls, where acidic coal and great silt-ridden dams and plutonium produce the electricity that keeps this house bright at night. I don't like being reminded of that connection. I'd prefer that it be hidden, for the lights to go on as if by magic.

Like John Rember, I know how exciting it was when the Rural Electrification Administration strung its poles down through the Judith River breaks in 1946 and brought us the possibility of instant light from a bare bulb hanging from the kitchen ceiling. I remember the fascination of a flush toilet; not that we owned one, but relatives did, and I thought that nothing could be more wonderful than a handle that pushed down, followed by a gush of water, and that no luxury could be better than not having to trek from a warm bed to an outhouse through rain or snow.

But nostalgia is a bad risk for any writer. I look back at my description, in *All but the Waltz*, of haying season in central Montana in the 1940s. I wrote it knowing that my own children had little idea of the work that once seemed so mundane to me, but I am struck now by my wistfulness:

> Haying season . . . is a water bottle clinking with diminishing ice, coated with bits of leaf and grass and fine pulverized dust in its shady uncut corner of the meadow. A shower of sparks and a shriek from the grinder from the log shed where my father is sharpening sickles. Meals of cold fried chicken and potato salad thrown on the table by my mother, who has dashed in from a day on the buck rake. But haying season belongs to the men. Their dirty slanted Stetsons and grimed faces, white teeth and hand-rolled cigarettes. The texture of their voices, the way their Levi's fit, the way they ride the mowers with their legs braced and their gloved hands full of lines. Their glamor.

Historical reconstruction has for years been the task of many writers in the West. Their purpose has been, according to Jon Tuska, to restore "man in nature, not the denatured, mechanical, sterile world that increasingly has come to serve as a backdrop of human activity in other kinds of fiction"; or, according to Greg Morris, "to reinterpret the historical circumstance of the West and, thereby, the nation," citing as examples Ron Hansen, Molly Gloss, and Ivan Doig.

Ivan Doig and I grew up in Montana on far-apart ranches and—although we knew nothing of each other—graduated from Montana high schools in the same year. Many of Ivan's memories stir mine, like his lovingly detailed descriptions in his novel *English Creek* of putting up hay with a homemade power buckrake made from an old automobile chassis and engine with a fork mounted on it to buck the hay from the fields to the stacks. Doig is a scrupulous researcher. When his *English Creek* narrator describes a scatter rake as "a long axle—mine was a ten-foot type—between a set of iron wheels [which] . . . carries a row of long thin curved teeth, set about a hand's width apart from each other, and it is this regiment of teeth that rakes along the ground and scrapes together any stray hay lying there," we can be certain that that is just what a scatter rake looked like and how it worked. But Doig's care, his exactitude, and his attention to detail in these descriptions only emphasize that his scene is already so remote that it must be documented.

Nostalgia? Only, I think, in his loving attention to detail. But many of Doig's readers will find here not memories, or historical documentation, or even, in his description of that first power buckrake, an inkling of the coming transformation of labor-intensive family ranch work into full mechanization and the economics of agribusiness. Rather, they are likely to expect, and find, the romance of the past.

"My people sent me to the desert as a child so I would learn how to work," writes William Kittredge, who has anchored his own reinterpretation of western history in the wanton and far-flung ranching and farming kingdoms of his own family, whose past he sees as anything but romantic. "My life since has been colored by what I got from four or five summers with . . . adults who in fundamental and goodhumored ways were willing to spend their time and lives absolutely on the topic at hand, whether gentling horses or braiding rawhide ropes, with even-handed intelligence." Kittredge, who advises creative writing students to write about real work in their fiction, has had to look for his kind of work in the past or in remote pockets of the West. When he discovers that some (how many?) of the old desert cow outfits are refitting their horse-drawn chuck wagons for what they say are economic reasons, he is heartened, although his cost-counting seems perfunctory. "What it comes to is rediscovering reasons for doing the work," he writes in *Owning It All.*

But work without an economic reason becomes something other than work. An avocation, perhaps, or a ritual. The ranch with the refitted horse-drawn chuck wagons becomes a dude ranch without guests, run for the entertainment of its owners and employees. "Should the [power] lines ever be buried," writes

John Rember, "the road now designated Scenic Highway 75 will look very much like it did in 1956. . . . Some of us who live here will be out digging ditch or fixing fence or working with the horses. Perhaps a bit of pageantry can be detected in our motions."

There lives today a rancher in the lush Deer Lodge Valley of Montana who still bucks in his hay with teams of horses and stacks it with a beaver slide within clear view of Interstate 90. Because haying season in the Deer Lodge Valley corresponds to the height of tourist season, it is not uncommon to find several cars pulled off the highway and several cameras clicking away at the spectacle of the two harnessed and sweating horses and the old man on the seat of his buckrake in his grimy working clothes. Is he oblivious of his audience?

Again, John Rember:

> There are worse lives than those lived in museums. There are worse shortcomings than a lack of authenticity. Trouble with unreality is much preferable to trouble with reality. So I get up in the morning, open the doors to the sun and tree-cleaned air and a river next door that has never known a discharge of treated effluent, look up at mountains that tear holes in the clouds, watch the eagle that has made this stretch of river his home this winter, and consider myself among the luckiest of men. But that's because the place I live in now reminds me that once I had a home in Sawtooth Valley when the fish were wild in the rivers, when our neighbors had always been cowboys and when a flip of the switch brought wonderful, magical, incredible light.

Rember may be right. There may be worse lives than those lived in museums. But I am a writer, and I am committed to probing my past and my present. What if I am doomed to inauthenticity?

Wallace Stegner once called the remaining western wilderness "the geography of hope," although, he noted near the end of his life, it may represent the "wrong kinds of hope." What Stegner had in mind was the continuing cult of individualism and the myth of the Garden of the West, which, he warned, would destroy what is left of our environment and blind us to the kinds of connections that Kittredge and others have urged that we make with each other and with landscape. In "Variations on a Theme by Crevecoeur," Stegner nominated some native-born writer—"some Doig or Hugo or Maclean or Welch or Kittredge or Raymond Carver"—as the new western hero, one who would transcend his culture without abandoning it, and who would find intimacy and interdependence in shared communities, shared optimism, and shared memory.

As if in answer to Stegner's challenge, recent writers in the West have taken part in a grand shift away from the old stories of the frontier that most of us grew up reading or hearing about. Elliott West points out that the new western fiction writers have been working at reinterpretation of the past in parallel with the new western historians. Greg Morris cites a dozen writers who "seek both to demolish myth and create myth anew." Alexander Blackburn, drawing from the tables of contents of several new anthologies of western writing, comes up with a list too long to quote in support of his argument that an honorific like "renaissance" is not inappropriate for the state of writing in the West. What we can celebrate in such a rich list is its diversity: the voices of Blackfeet, Chippewa, Sioux, Chinese-Americans, second-generation Finns, the sons of great ranching empires, the sons and daughters of starved-out homesteaders, young men and women who have grown up on reservations and in logging camps, on poultry farms and on faceless urban streets. The stories they tell are multitudinous, and we can be glad of the many strands where once we believed we had only one or two.

Still, in many ways we are a rear guard, writing as though we lived a century before cyberspace was ever considered. Greg Morris says that what we have in common is a conservative style. Many western writers, he argues,

> *want* to believe in the sacred and meaningful relationship between language and the land, because the Old West writers

believed in that relationship—it is their link to that tradition, and their means to the source of that tradition's power; but the radical and profound changes worked upon the Western landscape now make such belief difficult. So the New West writers settle for a style that allows a compromise, one that perhaps provides a new rhythm for an altered, abused landscape.

But while the literary link between living western writers and the recently dead—Edward Abbey, A. B. Guthrie, Jr., Norman Maclean, Wallace Stegner—is profound, it does not completely account for our connections between language and landscape. When creation myth overlies landscape, as it does for many Native American writers, the relationship between language and the land is literally sacred. Landscape may be so emotionally charged with a writer's reflection of self that James Welch, for example, can allow his main character in *The Indian Lawyer* to "see into the life of things" in an almost Wordsworthian sense, carrying the stark beauty of the prairie and its creatures—hawk, antelope, rattlesnake—with him in memory wherever he goes.

Too, for many of us, the western landscape is permeated with private associations contained in memory and family narratives. Language is how we move from private silence to shared story.

None of us wants to think about the death of landscape, and nostalgia may suffice some of us for a few more years. But we are not the first writers on earth to experience loss. While we fight for the preservation of the last wilderness areas (and allow ourselves to forget that "preservation," as Keats knew, implies a kind of death), as writers we should remember that in story lies possibility.

Meanwhile, back in the plastic world, much is going badly for the writer of the paved street. Sven Birkets deplores the monochrome nature of experience that confronts the postmodernist writer from the moment he wakens to the sound of his clock radio, shaves to the background noise of television, heats his breakfast in the microwave, gets in his car, and punches the button that activates his electric garage door. Off to work on the expressway, parking his car in an underground garage, taking an elevator up to his office, where he checks his e-mail. "The long day unfolds in carpeted and climate-controlled rooms, under the crackle of fluorescents. . . . And as the sun sets over the glass towers of his metropolis, he hurries home to a casserole, some Nintendo with the kids, and a few cold ones in front of *NYPD Blue*. There are days, quite a few in fact, when our man does not set foot in what used to be known as the outdoors."

As a fiction writer, what are you to do with such unpromising material? Birkets suggests that you might look for language that accurately depicts its depletion. Or you might mock, or ironize, or intrude imaginative havoc. You might, as Robert Stone does, set your character afloat on the high seas. But your most likely next move, says Birkets, will be to change the subject, because, he insists, literature must become dangerous again. Literature must lead us back toward a reconnaissance of selfhood. "You move into the past, into the 1950s or 1960s, say; or you betake yourself to some more rural place where the mediation is not yet so total."

In other words, you will travel west. Along with other fugitives from the paved streets, you will enroll in a graduate course in nonfiction creative writing at one of the western universities, and you will distress your instructor with essays about your backpacking trip into the wilderness wherein you found your soul in solitude. You will recognize, adore, and perhaps fight to save the depleted remnants of old-growth forest and unplowed grassland and the last wild salmon and the last bears, and you will be right to do so.

What you may not recognize is that the wilderness where you have come to look for your soul is already a museum. You will have mistaken our nostalgia for authenticity. It may take you years to learn, as it has us, that between Wallace Stegner and

Sven Birkets lies an contradiction. It will be hard for us to be romantic individuals, testing the depth of our despair against the frontier, and be responsible men and women of the twentieth century at the same time.

I cannot reconcile myself to the loss of landscape, which for me often is an analogy for my own body, sometimes even an extension of my body, like a outer membrane. And yet I know that I have never owned the landscape.

Any summer afternoon from the top of Main Street Hill you can see the tree-shaded streets of Lewistown, Montana, forty-five degrees off the true north, like a last legacy from those old Métis, the half-breeds who, years before my great-grandfather came west, had traveled out of the Red River country and down from Canada in the aftermath of the first Riel rebellion to build their cottonwood log cabins on the slope where the drain of a kitchen sink would eventually become the center of the state of Montana, and to plant gardens and orchards along the creek bottom and, as an afterthought, to lay out cattywampus streets between their fruit trees.

In time, 150 families of Métis had settled along Spring Creek. They were sedate in comparison with the white frontiersmen of the mining and wolving camps who were their neighbors, and they must have had their dreams, perhaps not as ambitious as my great-grandfather's dream of the Garden of the West, perhaps not so reasoned as Wallace Stegner's dream of responsible connections with each other and with place. Perhaps they did only what came next as it seemed best. They opened a school in Lewistown in 1881, began the construction of a Catholic church in 1886, and in 1903 sent for nuns to run the school and the St. Joseph's Hospital. Nuns were still running that hospital in 1939 when I was born there, and in 1959 when my first child was born there.

On their journey down to central Montana, the Métis had encountered the Nez Perce with Chief Joseph, fleeing toward their final stand in the Bear's Paw Mountains. Maybe they saw Blackfeet or Crow hunting parties, or met relatives among the Chippewa and the Cree. They were not eager to draw attention to themselves. Some of them may have fought and been betrayed in the first Riel rebellion, in 1870. After they settled on Spring Creek, they may have hosted an exiled Louis Riel himself before Gabriel Dumont rode down from Saskatchewan in 1885 to urge him to lead the half-breeds in their second, and bloodier and more disastrous, revolt against Canada.

As a child I never heard a word of Métis history. The descendants of the Métis themselves were known, in our Protestant world, as Catholic *breeds*, to distinguish them from Catholic middle-European *bohunks*. I went to school with a Métis girl called Donna LaFountain, who was ridiculed by cheerleaders for wearing cowboy boots under her skirts. Who could have supposed that Donna's boots and skirts would become fashionable in Aspen, Jackson Hole, Taos, Sun Valley?

Who could have supposed that our world might have been otherwise?

North of Lewistown, over the tops of the cottonwoods and beyond the Judith Mountains, the gray hills and hollows of the prairie stretch out of sight. Draws and coulees break the superimposed grid of ripening wheat and summer fallow. Chokecherry brush and groves of aspens along the creeks offer occasional shelter all the way to the breaks of the Missouri River along the old Carroll Trail.

Across this landscape in 1885, in Métis settlements and Indian camps at ten- or twenty-mile intervals along the 450-mile trail between Lewistown, Montana, and Regina, Saskatchewan, Gabriel Dumont set up secret relay stations with fresh horses by which he hoped to spirit Louis Riel down across the border to sanctuary in the Judith Basin after he had broken him out of jail in Regina. Captured after his second rebellion, Riel had been convicted of treason against Canada and was waiting to be hanged.

I might write this story for the glamour of a lost cause: how, somewhere out there, lost in distance, in the next coulee or in the ashes of a woodcutters' camp along the Missouri River, Gabriel Dumont still pursues his futile mission. The fleet horses and provisions wait, the rifles are ready. If he can just get Riel as far as the first of his camps, he can evade capture for a long time—but first, there is the matter of the heavily guarded Regina jail.

Or I might write as a historical reconstruction how Riel was hanged for treason on November 16, 1885, and how that was the end of a dream of a native state carved out of Canada and named Assiniboia.

But I continue to believe that in story lies possibility. Soon enough, as Sven Birkets fears, we may all erase our individual selves as we are hooked into the great circuits of cyberspace. We may lose the last remnants of the geography of hope. But stories need not be romantic, or despairing, or simplistic, or single-voiced. Stories need not even reflect landscape. Stories, in their search for common ground, can find the links between Métis history and the great-granddaughter of a land surveyor for the homestead frontier. Stories can be collective.

I tell my students, find your story. Follow it west, if that's where it leads you—chauvinistic talk about western "carpet-bagger" writers has more to do with territorial imperative than it does with literary merit, and many writers from "outside" see us more clearly than we see ourselves—but if it leads you home, don't be surprised. Recognize pageantry when you see it, but remember, as Annick Smith insists, that life is motion. Keep in touch with your friends. Treasure the place where you live and treat it tenderly.

Within the Rough-Edged Circle

I DAHO SPRAWLS OVER AN ENORMOUS TERRITORY, NOT
as large in square miles as Montana but at least as daunting
to travel across, partly because of its shape, which is roughly
a capital *L*, or perhaps the outline of a miner's boot, as some
suggest, and partly because of the national forests and the fabulous wilderness areas—the Selway-Bitterroot, the Gospel Hump,
the Frank Church–River of No Return, the Sawtooth—that separate the southern part of the state from the north. The drive
from Porthill, at the northernmost tip of Idaho's panhandle,
down to Montpelier, in the southeast corner near the Wyoming
border, is nearly eight hundred miles. When I first lived in
Lewiston, at the base of the panhandle, I had to get out an atlas
to convince myself that the distance between me and my older
daughter, Elizabeth, in St. Anthony, near the Tetons, was greater
than it had been when I lived in Havre, Montana.

On our first Memorial Day weekend in Idaho, I took Rachel
and went to visit Elizabeth, taking Highway 95—the north-and-
south "goat trail," as it's often called—through Lawyer Canyon
and across the Camas Prairie, through Grangeville and down the
sheer, teetering grade on White Bird Hill, where, in 1877, a force
of soldiers and white volunteers attacked a band of nontreaty

Nez Perce under Chief Joseph and sparked the war. After White Bird, Highway 95 follows the sparkling twists and whitewater rapids of the Salmon River. Sheer basalt cliffs rise up from the ancient lava bedrock, cast their sharp-edged shadows, and break into white pine and tamarack that reach toward the peaks with the beautiful names. The Lemhi Range, the Lost River Range. The river town of Riggins sprawls along the edge of the national forest, its bars and motels and the establishments of outfitters lining the highway, its houses perched on the steep sides of hills. Another thirty miles and the river valley broadens at New Meadows, where north-south travelers usually take Highway 55 to Boise and suddenly remember that they've lost an hour, because they've just crossed the line between Pacific and Mountain time zones.

For several of the summers that I've lived in Idaho, Highway 55 between New Meadows and Boise has been closed because of forest fires, requiring a long detour around by Weiser. But on that first trip, I drove straight through McCall, on Payette Lake, and on up through Horseshoe Bend to Boise, and joined Interstate 84 on its long sweep across southern Idaho, where the land changes from mountains to high desert. Miles of sagebrush, miles of potato farms, population strung like beads along the highway. Mountain Home. Jerome. American Falls, Blackfoot, Idaho Falls. It was dark when we pulled into St. Anthony, and I had to call Elizabeth to come and guide us to the house in the country where she was living.

At the end of our visit, I decided to drive home through Montana and see whether it took any longer. Interstate 15 took us north across Monida Pass at an elevation of 6,823 feet, over high prairie to Dillon, Montana, with a storm blowing in behind us. By the time we turned west on Interstate 90 to Missoula, the wet snow was coming down in globs and traffic was crawling, or stalled, or spinning across both lanes to land in the ditch. I kept pulling off on the shoulder and unclogging my windshield wipers with my bare fingers, waving off the occasional highway patrolman who rolled down his own snow-packed window and mouthed, *Are you okay?*

I told Rachel that if the storm was worse when we got to Missoula, we would check into a motel—or I would call a friend and ask if we could stay the night—but we both wanted to get home, and it seemed to me that the snowfall was less dense as I took the familiar bypass around the university and headed for Lolo on Highway 12 with a crick in my neck from peering ahead to see through the windshield. I had been driving for—what, eight or nine hours by that time?—and snow kept falling through the bare groves of quaking aspen as the mountain slopes rose into pine forest. But it did seem to me that the snow was letting up, melting as it fell on the asphalt, fell into last fall's matted grass, fell and dissolved into the black cold of the river current. By the time we crossed the line into Idaho, at the top of Lolo Pass, it had changed to rain, and we had gained back our lost hour as we reentered the Pacific time zone. Another four hours, and we would be driving into Lewiston, past the pulp mill lit like a cruise ship and emitting its white puffs and wet-cabbage stench into the night sky, across the bridge on the Clearwater, and up the grade to the small house I had rented on the edge of the Lewiston Orchards. Then, with Rachel in bed, with a glass of whiskey at hand, I would look at the road atlas and realize that I had crossed the continental divide twice and driven in a giant, rough-edged circle, covering something close to fifteen hundred miles.

Given these distances, and the diverse topography of Idaho—mountains, deserts, rivers, high plateaus, and rolling prairie—it's no wonder that the state tends to divide itself into regions. I can drive from my home in Moscow to Missoula or Seattle or Spokane in less time than it takes to drive to Boise, the state capital, and in far less time than it takes to drive to Pocatello. Now that Horizon Air has cut back on its flights, I can't even fly from Moscow to Boise; I have to take the shuttle to Seattle and change planes. ("That's nothing," said Ford Swetnam, who teaches at Idaho State University in Pocatello. "We have to fly out of Pocatello on Delta to Atlanta and change planes there.")

So we have the mountainous panhandle, blessed by lakes and split by the Priest River and the Kootenai River, the Coeur d'Alene and the St. Joe. We have the Palouse, which spills from Moscow over into eastern Washington State. Down at the base of the panhandle, we have the Confluence, at the old territorial capital of Lewiston, where the Snake River and the Clearwater converge and flow westward toward the Columbia. East of Lewiston, facing Montana, we have the Selway-Bitterroot Wilderness with its rivers, the Lochsa and the Selway and the North Fork of the Clearwater. Beyond the vast central wilderness area, with New Meadows and McCall and Boise dotting its edges, is the Columbia Plateau and the Owyhee Desert, which stretches down toward Utah. Then the Snake River Plain and the Craters of the Moon and all the empty country with its population strung out along Interstate 84. Then the Targhee National Forest and the Caribou National Forest, which stretch over into Wyoming. We are something over a million people, spread out over 82,413 square miles.

Skiers tend to map out Idaho in terms of its winter resorts. Schweitzer Mountain, up in the panhandle. Brundage Mountain, near McCall. Bogus Basin, outside of Boise. And Soldier Mountain. And the really famous one, Sun Valley, just east of Ketchum. Academics, on the other hand, tend to read their map of Idaho in terms of colleges and universities. There's North Idaho College up in Coeur d'Alene, the University of Idaho here in Moscow, Lewis-Clark State College thirty miles down the road in Lewiston, and then, strung along the interstate in the southern part of the state, Northwest Nazarene College and Boise State University and Albertson College and Southern Idaho College and Ricks College. Finally, all the way down in Pocatello, is Idaho State University.

Given the size and shape of Idaho, I wondered whether I would ever get a real sense of the state. Over in Montana, they're fond of saying that everybody lives in the same small town with one awfully long street, and the saying has some truth. Everybody in Montana does seem to know each other. While they do divide their territory into eastern Montana (prairie, conservative) and western Montana (mountainous and dominated by the liberal-decadent professorate at the university in Missoula), and while writers in Montana tend either to be Missoula writers or else writers from other parts of the state who mutter darkly about a power clique I've actually heard described as Missoula-centric, most people in Montana do have some idea of what they mean when they call themselves *Montanans*.

People in Idaho don't usually call themselves *Idahoans* (a nineteenth-century missionary schoolteacher named Kate Macbeth campaigned hard for *Idahovans*, but the name never caught on). There is a diffidence in Idaho, a sense of amorphousness, as though in the minds of its residents the state has never been fully invented. If they can't find the words to describe themselves, perhaps in their own minds they don't quite exist. "I'm from Sun Valley," wrote one of my composition students, "and let me tell you, it's not what you think." But he was never able to explain what he meant.

What, I wondered, would it be like to be a writer in Idaho, to start all over without connections, without a sense of place, without a tradition? The only Idaho writers I had ever heard of (not counting Ezra Pound, who was born here, and Ernest Hemingway, who died here) were Vardis Fisher, whom I thought of as a pale reflection of A. B. Guthrie, writing historical novels about mountain men and Mormon settlers, and Carol Ryrie Brink, whose prize-winning children's novel, *Caddie Woodlawn*, I had loved, but whose adult novels I could not have named. But now here I was, with two cats and a five-year-old daughter and the odds and ends I had snatched out of the shards of a nightmare marriage, numb from ten years in higher ed administration, trying to pull together the shreds of what I remembered about teaching, and wondering if I would ever write again.

And here I still am. Rachel is fifteen now, and my foster daughter is sixteen, and we're up to four cats and a dog. Ironically, I have an office in Carol Ryrie Brink Hall.

I had been living in Idaho for several weeks when I was invited to dinner by the Brownings. Probably I had met Keith Browning earlier, although I don't remember. But—"Bring your little gal with you," Keith had urged, over the phone, and so Rachel and I drove through the Lewiston Orchards, where the heavy green foliage of sycamores and locusts and Oregon maples showed hardly a touch of fall frost, and I searched those narrow, perplexing streets for the address I had been given. Finally I found Hemlock Avenue, although it looked more like a graveled alley, even a cow path, and I followed it between horse pastures and trailer courts and newly constructed split-levels until I came to the right mailbox and pulled into the driveway between an overgrown lilac hedge and a grape arbor on a scrap of lawn. And there was Keith, massive and grizzled, beckoning to us from his kitchen steps.

The Brownings, Keith and Shirley, had come over from Oregon twenty years earlier to teach at the little state college in Lewiston. He had chaired the English department for a time, and Shirley had taught composition, and they both threw their energies into the place they had made home. They taught full schedules, they brought up their two children, they started a lecture series that continues to this day, they started a poets-in-the-schools program, and, in a utility room opening off their kitchen, they founded Confluence Press.

When I first met them, they were newly retired. They had turned the press over to a new director, they were looking forward to doing some traveling, and Keith thought he might revise his novel for publication. Meanwhile they enjoyed the company of their friends. Shirley had been stricken with polio at the age of seven, and she navigated her own home with the aid of a walker and drove her car, but she found it less tiring when her friends came to her, so she and Keith entertained often. None of this I knew, that first afternoon, when Keith ushered Rachel and me into a spacious room full of clear Idaho light that fell through floor-to-ceiling windows. And there was Shirley on her couch, in her red sweater, white-haired and smiling—"Do you play Scrabble?" she asked me. "Oh, lovely!"

I have visited the Brownings so many times during the past ten years that it is hard to sort out the details of that first visit. In fact, it's hard to imagine that there was a first time. I pull into that familiar driveway, I'm bear-hugged by Keith, I'm struck all over again by the flood of light and the feeling that I've come home. While I'm greeting Shirley with a kiss, Keith is pouring me a George Dickel, and I take the drink and sit in one of the sprawling blue easy chairs by the windows that open the living room to a deck and then the hills that roll all the way to the tips of Oregon's Blue Mountains and the endless, blowing sky. "Helluva view," Keith says, and it is.

For several of the years that I have been visiting the Brownings, Keith's sister Marg lived with them. Marg was the oldest of the ten Browning brothers and sisters from an Oregon stump farm, and Keith was the youngest. She had helped to raise the rest of the clan, and they were all devoted to her. When I first met her, she was past ninety and frail. She tottered about her small household tasks, greeted friends—"Always so good to see you, dear," she would say, and pat my hand—then doze in her chair, fading in and out of the conversation that she loved. When I brought my visiting Aunt Sylva, then in her mid-eighties, down to meet Marg, the two women immediately became absorbed in talk of their own, as animated as two teenagers who'd been isolated from their peers for months and finally found each other. Shirley and I listened, elated by their rapport and Marg's rekindled sparkle, but silenced—at least, I was—at witnessing the loneliness of old age, the hunger for the companionship and understanding of a contemporary.

When Marg died, Keith and Shirley took her home to Oregon, where she was given an enormous funeral, attended by the friends and sons and daughters of the sprawling Browning family and by the children and grandchildren of her many students from her days as a high school English teacher. Then Keith and Shirley came back to Idaho and invited their friends to a private memorial. We sat in a circle in the Browning living room, wept and drank wine, reminisced and read aloud the poems we each had written for Marg.

Lewiston is the old territorial capital of Idaho. Its main street is as narrow and crooked as it was in the days when Lewiston was the supply camp for the gold mines, and provisions and equipment were brought by steamboat up the Columbia River from Portland, unloaded here, and packed on mules to be humped up the trails along the Clearwater to Orofino and Pierce and over Lolo Pass into Montana. Those days have been gone for over a hundred years, but the street meanders and winds past the ornate old nineteenth-century three-story facades and the new banks and renovations and fountains and parks, hard against the bluff of Normal Hill, where you can still see the rifle pits dug by frightened citizens in 1877 when they thought the fugitive Nez Perce might attack Lewiston instead of fleeing over Lolo to the Big Hole.

Spring comes to Lewiston earlier than it does anywhere else in the northern Rockies. In the shelter of those stark hills where the rivers pour together into the Confluence, the air softens and the cherries bloom in March. The willows along the river are changing from golden to pale green, and the shade trees in their ornamental iron cages on Main Street are on the verge of leafing out. Next month it will be the dogwoods and lilacs in clouds of purple and pink and white all over town. Meanwhile, even at dusk a balminess hangs over the streets. I'm always amazed at the difference in climate down here from up on the Palouse where I live now, only thirty miles to the north but about a thousand feet higher in elevation.

Tonight, after a dinner at the Brownings, I've driven downtown with the poet Neidy Messer, from Boise, and parked on D Street, across from the Center for the Arts and History, which the local college administers in a renovated bank building. It's a little after seven. The streetlights are beginning to glow, and the kids and the kickers and the cowboys are revving up their cars and four-wheel-drive pickups for their Saturday night cruising, up D Street, around the loop, and down Main, over and over infinitely into the night. For now, the traffic isn't bad, just the occasional screech of tire from a block away, a few yips back and forth from open windows. Neidy and I cross the street and enter what once was a bank lobby but now is an expansive room with high, ornate windows and chandeliers, set up with a podium and tables and chairs for tonight's benefit reading.

Neidy and I are a bit early, but others follow. Here's the bunch up from Pocatello, Fort Swetnam and Gino Sky and Harald Wyndham, who operates Blue Scarab Press. Bill Studebaker has driven four hundred miles from Twin Falls, Fay Wright has come all the way down from Coeur d'Alene. Besides Neidy from Boise, there's Rick Ardinger with his red hair and red beard, the executive director of the Idaho Humanities Commission and the proprietor and operator, along with his wife, Rosemary, of Limberlost Press. Here are Robert Wrigley and his wife, Kim Barnes, who have driven down the Clearwater from Lenore, and here is Gary Gildner, who lives in Grangeville now. Claire Davis lives in Lewiston and teaches fiction writing. Her husband, Dennis Held, is tonight's master of ceremonies when he can take time out from hawking subscriptions to the college's literary magazine, *Talking River Review.*

This evening's reading is being held in honor of Marg, in whose name Keith and Shirley have established a scholarship fund for creative writing students at Lewis-Clark State College.

Of course Keith is here, pushing a festive Shirley in the wheel-chair she has been relegated to for the past year or so. Also their son, Chris, and Keith's brother Dan and his wife. Also a crowd of students and former students and faculty. I'm greeting friends, being hugged by people I haven't seen for a month or so, chatting with some of my MFA students down from Moscow. Eventually everybody settles down and Dennis Held manages to tear himself loose and get up to the podium—"It's going to be ten o'clock before we're finished!" worries Kim Barnes from across our table.

In fact, it will be nearly eleven.

Listening while these twelve people from all over Idaho read from their work, I realize that the evening is turning into a testimonial for Keith and Shirley Browning. Harald, Bill, Rick, Fay, and Neidy recall that it was the Brownings who published their first chapbooks at Confluence Press, or who published their poems in the now-defunct *Slackwater Review* and told them yes! You're a writer, and words matter, and you must keep writing!

I am particularly struck when Bill Studebaker gets up to read some of his new poems about kayaking—he explains that, in a given year, he spends about a hundred and twenty days on the river—and he thanks the Brownings and also the many people in the room who have offered him help, criticism, and encouragement. And I think about what I've been learning for the past ten years; that yes, I have been able to write here, and yes, this is a generous place.

Can the efforts of one or two persons influence the quality of writing in an entire state or region? The current wealth of Montana writers often is traced back to the efforts of H. G. Merriam, who, following his appointment as an instructor of English at the University of Montana in 1919, nurtured and encouraged a generation of regional writers, established the second creative writing program in the United States, and founded the magazines *Frontier* and *Midland*, which gave his protégés an opportunity to showcase their work. One of Merriam's students was Dorothy M. Johnson, who appropriated the old dime-novel mystique and rendered its cowboys and Indians more stylishly than anyone before or since. Another of his students was A. B. Guthrie, Jr., and another was D'Arcy McNickle, the Métis novelist who wrote *The Surrounded* and *Wind from an Enemy Sky*. Over the years, the creative writing program that Merriam founded has attracted teacher-writers as remarkable and diverse as Walter Van Tilburg Clark, Leslie Fiedler, Richard Hugo, and William Kittredge, who in turn influenced a younger generation.

Indeed, a disproportionate number of the current Idaho writers hold MFA degrees from the University of Montana. So why such a difference in the way we think of ourselves and our work, as though the state boundary line along the tips of the mountains were a real barrier?

Any regional writer begins with certain advantages: a narrowing down of the bewildering multiplicity of the American experience, a precise sense of place, a dramatic history on which to draw. The dilemma for these writers, a quandary which is particularly poignant for native writers, is that, however centered they may be in their own territory, they write for an audience which is likely to perceive their region as marginal. This wider audience still looks for news of the exotic, the uncommon, still hankers for local color. The writer's risk is in being patronized as quaint, and those of us who write about the West will forever be, in Sherman Alexie's words, in the business of fancydancing.

In an essay that enraged many Montanans in 1949, Leslie Fiedler wrote, "When he admits that the Noble Savage is a lie; when he has learned that his state is where the myth comes to die . . . the Montanan may find the possibilities of tragedy and poetry for which so far he has searched his life in vain."

Forty years later, arguably the most distinguished writer in Montana is the Blackfeet James Welch, who was a student of

Richard Hugo's and was advised by Hugo to write about what he knew. The Oneida poet Roberta Hill Whiteman, who also studied with Hugo, the Fort Peck playwright William Yellow Robe, and the Salish fiction writer Debra Earling are among the most promising of the current generation of native writers. Here in Idaho we haven't heard as much from the Nez Perce or the Coeur d'Alenes or the Bannack and Shoshones, although we do try to claim Janet Campbell Hale and Sherman Alexie.

But Idaho is not Montana. In spite of our close literary and historical connections—Montana, after all, was sliced off the old Idaho Territory as a "geographical impossibility," as its historians put it, in 1864—Idaho is unique. The subtle differences of colors, the shadows on bare river bluffs, the plunge of rivers down the western face of the divide remind me every day that I'm living in Idaho and nowhere else. Our backs are against the mountains here, and our eyes follow the broadening flow of the Columbia to the Pacific.

What we have here in Idaho is less tradition and a lower profile. An MFA program that is perhaps the newest in the United States and certainly one of the smallest. A couple of chronically underfunded university presses and a smattering of hand letterpresses, like Limberlost and Blue Scarab. A few people working overtime, like Sandy Ashworth up in Bonner's Ferry, who directs the newly formed Idaho Writers Connection, and Tom Trusky at Boise State University, who directs the Idaho Center for the Book, and Clay Morgan in McCall, who organizes the annual Readers and Writers Rendezvous. Half a dozen independent bookstores that will sponsor readings and stock the works of local writers.

Idaho is marked by isolation: isolation between the races, isolation between north and south, and the psychic isolation of our deep differences in politics and religion and economics. Its isolation is intensified by that fifteen-hundred-mile circle that it still takes to drive around the state.

But when the writers begin to emerge from their enclaves,

when they're willing to take time from their own work to drive up to ten or twelve hours to take part in a benefit reading for an old friend, when they read each other's work and offer the words of encouragement and appreciation that sometimes are all we've got to keep us going, then we know we're on the cusp of something. As Keith Browning says, it's a helluva view from here.

All writers must work in solitude. But if Idaho remains largely uninvented, it's up to us to find the words for the place where we live, and we'll be the better for joining the circle, offering community as the respite that every solitary writer needs.

Queen Moo of Mayax

I N THESE LATE YEARS I'VE COME TO ANOTHER RIVER,
where gold light falls on the Snake in the afternoon, and the
current looks almost solid enough to walk across. It is a dangerous illusion, because here at Buffalo Eddy the river is at its
most treacherous. Back before the Lower Granite and Hells
Canyon dams were built, this stretch of the Snake erupted out
of Hells Canyon in a turmoil of whirlpools that swallowed logs,
boats, bodies, spat out some of them downstream, kept others
forever. This afternoon's quiet surface may seem serene as it
reflects the sun and patches of deep buff and olive from the willow leaves on the opposite bank, but deep down under the tons
of water, the whirlpools still churn and spin their ancient plun-
der, sticks and bones.

Although I knew that the petroglyphs at Buffalo Eddy
were one of the largest sites of rock art in the Columbia
Plateau, I looked for a long time before I saw them. The ones
I finally spotted were human forms etched into the basalt
rocks on the opposite side of the river, two or three feet high
and nearly white against the dark surface. Often they were
grouped in threes, a large figure and two lesser ones. Curiously
thick-bodied, with inadequate-looking legs but with massive

arms, they brandished objects that resembled barbells, or batons.

Seeing them like that for the first time, without having them pointed out to me, was as though the figures had floated up from some murky rock depths. They had always been there, etched into the face of the basalt, and yet they had suddenly materialized before my eyes. I looked at them for a long time from my side of the river, unwilling to take my eyes off them lest they vanish again.

It was weeks, even months later, on another visit to Buffalo Eddy, that I clambered out on the basalt boulders that thrust into the river current, glanced down, and saw petroglyphs under my feet. Dozens of etchings, even hundreds, of human forms, brandishing their barbells, and animals with long, graceful legs and sweeping horns, and strange abstractions, coils and spirals, rows of dots and chains and zigzags that ran everywhere, over the sides and tops and flat surfaces of the boulders. I caught my breath, almost afraid to move. It was as though I had walked through a transparency and had my eyes opened in a world that lay parallel to the one I thought I knew.

Petroglyphs are rock engravings, created by pecking at the rock surface with a sharp piece of harder stone, or by using the harder stone to rub or abrade the rough surface down to a smooth grain, or by scratching fine, light lines into a dark rock surface. They have been found all over the world, in France and Spain, in Australia, in sites all over North America. Dating rock art is difficult, but some of the oldest petroglyphs in the Pacific Northwest depict hunters with spears or atlatls and dogs in pursuit of mountain sheep and may have been carved five thousand years ago. Others depict horses and riders and must have been carved since 1720, when Spanish horses first were traded as far north as the Columbia Plateau. Some, even more recent, depict sailing ships, firearms, and the occasional human figure in a broad European-style hat. A story told by the Native American novelist Mourning Dove, "A Mix-Up at Picture Rocks," has to do with a child who misinterprets a petroglyph carved in about 1862.

The petroglyphs at Buffalo Eddy are among the hundreds of rock art sites that still exist throughout the Columbia River drainage system in western Montana, British Columbia, Washington, and Oregon, and along the lower Snake River, which divides Idaho from Washington State. To find them, cross the bridge between Lewiston, Idaho, and Clarkston, Washington, and drive south on Washington State Highway 129 through the little town of Asotin, on the banks on the Snake. In a few miles, turn left on a gravel road that follows the river. The petroglyphs are visible from a car window for those who look long enough. I know where there are pictographs at the back of a shallow cave in the basalt cliffs, a few miles downstream from Buffalo Eddy on the Idaho side of the Snake River, but although most people who live at the Confluence know where they are, I won't give the directions. Wind and water erosion over hundreds and thousands of years has been less damaging to the rock art sites than the construction of dams and railroads and highways, but even dynamiting through the thousand-foot-depth of the basalt has often been less damaging than vandalism. Many sites have been defaced by paint or by somebody's initials freshly scratched over the old etchings or rock paintings, and at Buffalo Eddy I can see the scars on the basalt where, about fifteen years ago, somebody used a crowbar to pry loose a panel and haul it away.

Pictographs, as distinguished from petroglyphs, are painted on the face of the rock, usually with a red pigment made from crushed iron oxides mixed with blood or urine. They are likely to be found in hidden or inaccessible places, often in the form of a few images painted by a single artist, perhaps by someone on a vision quest. Compared with the petroglyphs, the Snake River pictographs seem very private to me. I feel out of place in their presence, as though I've interrupted a prayer. It isn't much of a stretch to imagine the young girl or the young man, hardly out of childhood, lying in the back of that cave and fasting into a dream state, then dipping a finger into the paint—and yes, the lines are just the width of a finger—to connect outward space and inward experience.

Unlike the carvings, which alter the surface of the rock, the pictographs actually transform themselves from one state to another. Canadian scientists, observing that the colors of the paint (usually red but sometimes yellow or black or white, or even blue-green) don't seem to fade over hundreds or even thousands of years, have discovered that the pigment gradually separates from its binding agent through the natural weathering process and stains the rock as it seeps into its pores. In effect, the painting becomes a part of the rock.

Beyond the obvious—that Pacific Northwest rock art usually depicts human, animal, and spirit figures like the ones that dance on the basalt boulders at Buffalo Eddy, and that these figures may be associated with rituals of religion, magic, and hunting—archaeologists have been reluctant to speculate on their meaning, or to offer interpretations. But the first question almost everybody else asks is, *What do they mean?*

Some of the carvings may record great events. Those horses and riders could represent Nez Perce war parties, returning from successful raids on the other side of the mountains. From old transcripts of oral accounts, we know that there were such raids, and we know they were sometimes commemorated in stone. Or some of the carvings might be messages left by travelers. *We went downriver. Look for us there.*

Other carvings may carry mythological significance. There's the broken circle surrounded by another circle, for example, with a flat head that might represent a coiled rattlesnake. It might be a warning. *Watch out!* Or it might be a version of an archetypal symbol found all over the world—the *uroborus*, container of opposites, yang and yin, alpha and omega.

Then there are the so-called tally marks, which are among

the most common of designs. Short, straight, horizontal lines like ladders without sides, carved or painted into the rock, consistent in their spacing and executed with a care that shows they're no mere doodling. Are the tallies a form of record-keeping, *so many salmon caught, so many deaths this winter, so many children born?* Are they ways of remembering rituals, as James Keyser suggests, like rosaries or the stations of the cross? Or could they contain personal memories, like the balls of knotted string that Métis women kept as diaries?

The most baffling of the petroglyphs are the carvings formally classified as geometric. Circles and whorls, crosses, dots arranged in lines or other patterns, chains, zigzags, and abstract designs make up almost half of all the examples of rock art ever documented in our southeastern part of the Columbia Plateau. After all, to call a design *abstract* implies that it was abstracted from something. For some, the geometrics contain tantalizing hidden messages, just beyond understanding—or maybe just within understanding, if we apply an inventive theory. Messages left by lost Celtic monks, for example, in an ancient script called Ogam. Or Viking runes that document Norse exploration of North America, all the way from the coast of present-day Newfoundland to Buffalo Eddy, on the Snake River in Idaho. Or codes and calculations blasted into the rock by prehistoric space travelers.

I find myself drawn most profoundly to the human figures. Often the pictographs are dim at first, then those long bodies seem to float to the surface as though the basalt were still the liquid lava that once flowed and buckled and broke from the force of an ancient eruption. Stick arms and legs begin to emerge, and heads, and breasts that levitate from either side, or disproportionately weighty penises that seem to drag the bodies back down toward the eternal whirlpools in the core of the rock. If ever art struggled to reconcile subject and object, motion and stasis, permanence and flux, this does; and I, who have long suffered the contradictions of double vision, of belonging in place and being out of place, feel a magnet's pull into that everlasting tension.

Unlike the slender, finger-width men and women who float out of the pictographs, the petroglyph people at Buffalo Eddy seem confrontational, threatening, with their massive triangular-shaped shoulders scraped out of the sheer basalt, their legs wide-spread in fighting stance, their long arms brandishing their barbells as if they're defending the doorway into the stone. And there are so many of them. I focus on the boldest of the figures, find my eyes sliding to another and another, smaller and smaller as though they are arranged in perspective, becoming more and more abstract, almost to the point of looking more like distorted crosses than human figures. Small graceful animals race below their feet, but the animals aren't being hunted, the petroglyph people aren't pursuing these elk and mountain sheep with bows or atlatls as they do in the painted scenes, they seem rather to be guarding them.

Guarding them from whom? From me?

We live on an ancient basalt plateau, formed by layers and layers of lava flow from successive volcanic eruptions during the Miocene period, between ten and thirty million years ago. Further upriver from Buffalo Eddy, the basalt cliffs rise more than a thousand feet as the Snake River boils and froths its way through Hells Canyon. Twenty miles downstream from here, the basalt turns columnar, which is to say that it appears to have been shaped by some giant hand into huge, hexagonal tubes that suggest the pipes of some colossal cathedral organ or—to me— petrified motion. It's as though all that boiling hot lava spurted through the fingers of the gods a split second ago and froze into those contorted shapes. Surely if I glance over my shoulder, if I let my eyes fall out of focus and snap them back fast enough, I'll catch molten, fluid rock in the act of congealing.

But here, below the petroglyph boulders, the broad current of the Snake flows in a tranquility that belies all turmoil. Over on the Idaho side, scrub locust and grass climb away from the river through broken basalt toward the sun. Often I've seen cattle grazing there, sometimes I've seen deer, and further up the canyon I've seen mountain sheep with horns just like the ones carved under my feet. It's peaceful here. Traffic on the gravel road behind me is infrequent, usually local people going fishing. Sometimes the big cruise boat from Beamers Landing chugs by with a load of sightseers who are having the rock carvings on the Idaho side of the river pointed out to them, but not today. The splash and little V of parting water might be an otter swimming against the current, more likely a muskrat. I'd try to persuade myself that time itself has stopped, but I know that I could poke around among these rocks and find crushed beer cans, condoms, trash.

Sometimes I've brought friends to Buffalo Eddy, and only once I've regretted it. Not that he was a vandal, he was just a man I was in love with, but he saw the river and the rocks and the carvings through a filter, and I never saw them the same way again. Not that I was without complicity, I had brought him because I wanted him to see me here. I was committing the old cultural sin of westerners and pandering place.

According to the cultural geographers, narrative is a way of bringing our split vision of the world back into focus. It closes the distance between story and storyteller, between the rock and the concept of the rock. Maybe it's this stretch that accounts for some of the taller tales associated with the petroglyphs.

The tallest of these tales that I've heard has to do with the three lost continents of Mu, whose former existence in the Pacific Ocean a Colonel James Churchward believed he had discovered evidence for in certain "ancient tabloids," whatever these might be. *Three* lost continents put legends of a single lost continent of Atlantis to shame, and Churchward believed more:

that the population of Mu had divided itself into ten tribes, that these ten tribes had set out from their homeland to colonize the world, and that they carried with them a universal language which, properly interpreted, can be read in the abstract designs carved into rocks like the ones at Buffalo Eddy in Idaho.

Recently I came upon an account of the amateur archaeologist Harold J. Cundy, who for years studied and recorded the rock art of the Columbia Plateau. It seems that when Cundy read Churchward's book *The Lost Continent of Mu*, he realized that, in Muvian symbolism, he had found the key to understanding many carvings and paintings that had long puzzled him.

Cundy was a flour salesman for what would later become Centennial Flour Mills in Wenatchee, Washington. He had traveled all over central Washington on his sales route and followed up every local report of "Indian picture writing" that he came across. His notes and his loving and detailed drawings, done in pencil at the sites and sometimes recopied in ink and watercolor at home, are still an important source of information about rock art sites long covered by water after the building of the dams or dynamited away during road building. His drawings of the unique petroglyphs and pictographs at Picture Rocks Bay are particularly valuable; this site contained more than three hundred separate figures and abstractions that were among the most powerful and dramatic ever recorded along the Columbia River, including many of the mysterious "twin" representations, human figures wearing rayed arcs and circles like haloes around their heads, herds of mountain sheep, and curious, unexplained lines and other configurations. Cundy's drawings and a few photographs are all that is left of this trove. In 1964, the rising waters behind Wanapum Dam covered Picture Rocks Bay.

Muvian symbolism, however, seems to have provided Cundy with the kind of inspiration that Archimedes got from his overflowing bathtub, or Newton from his falling apple, or Joseph Smith from the golden tablets that explained how the ten lost tribes of Israel became the Indians of America. Studying Churchward's texts, Cundy suddenly realized that one of the unusual petroglyphs at Picture Rocks was a representation of Queen Moo of Mayax, wearing a curious arrangement of lines above her head that makes her look, in Cundy's drawing, like the queen of an ant colony with three antennae. In her left hand she grips an implement that resembles a rake, or perhaps a trident; in her right hand she holds an even stranger object that spews lines over the rayed circles at her feet. Carved into the rock on either side of the queen's head are more symbols, connected by a bar which she seems to be clenching in her teeth. Perhaps she's preparing for her trip to Egypt, where, according to Churchward, she caused the Sphinx to be built as a monument to her husband.

Here at the placid surface, where the river deepens with the reflections of leaves and spreads its slow gold current in the late sun, as I sit on these warm black boulders in the company of the dancing sheep and the spirals and whorls and the watchful petroglyph people with their barbells held aloft, it occurs to me to wonder how the queen got to Egypt. Perhaps she sailed by raft or canoe—many of the Pacific Northwest rock art sites show curved lines filled with smaller, vertical lines like the teeth in a comb, which are generally supposed to represent people in canoes—or perhaps she used a more direct route. Perhaps anticipating the individual who, about twenty years ago, so strongly believed that a certain set of pictographs contained coded instructions to open a door through the rock into another dimension that he defaced the site with red paint to warn unwary travelers, the queen spoke her password to her guards and descended through the sliding panels in the rock to the other side of the world. If that's the case, it's little wonder that those dozens of human figures with their sturdy, triangular bodies and their menacing arms keep watch over their basalt portals after so many hundreds, even thousands, of years.

Whatever narratives the rock art sites contain, neither fanciful spinning nor sober guesswork based on scientific calculation is likely to reveal them now, and I'm sitting this afternoon in the middle of what the theorists call the cognitive gap, in a world that has finally gotten so complex that it eludes our best efforts to locate ourselves in place or to connect our subjective perceptions of place with a measurable external landscape. Except in parody or in a paroxysm of self-consciousness, I can't dip my fingers in paint made from crushed iron oxide and my own urine and draw the lines between my dream vision and the solid rock. I can't merge with my narrative and stand outside it at the same time. But for a little while I can sit here in the late afternoon sunlight of Idaho in autumn, I can listen to the river in the company of the petroglyph people, I can respect their silence.

The Daughters in Summer

I HAVE LIVED FOR FOUR YEARS NOW IN THIS SMALL
university town at the base of the Idaho panhandle on the
edge of mountains that gradually descend into the low
rolling hills of the Palouse. My home is a rambling brown frame
house in what used to be the outskirts of town. Housing developments have sprung up around us in past years, but Paradise
Creek flows between backyards here, and wheatfields abut the
end of our street. My windows are filled with leaves. Poplars
tremble outside my study; cottonwoods and maples and willows
hang over the creek, filter the light, and cast their flickering patterns across my deck. In the afternoons I can almost believe in a
life of peace and quiet.

From here the sun rises out of the national forests of the
Bitterroots, travels west, and strews gold across the wheatfields
that for the past hundred years have replaced the deep grass
and sparse pines of old Nez Perce hunting grounds. Seasons
change color as the wheat sprouts, ripens, and is harvested.
Tranquility rests on the surface here, especially at midsummer
when the college students, for the most part, have gone back
to their home towns and shade hangs deep over the residential
streets.

Soon enough the students will be back and the issues of our time will flare up: the cutting of timber in the national forests, the flooding of small creeks and overburdened rivers over eroded banks, the depletion of topsoil on the Palouse. I know more about these threats from the newspapers or talk in class than I do in my bones. This isn't my landscape, I don't know its inner secrets and curves, although I know it has its stories, which I can surmise. Every gully, every creek on the Palouse has its history, and today the up-to-date green and white county road signs proclaim *Bear Creek Road, Dead Steer Road, Russian Road*. Behind these signs lie the older names that the Nimipu, the Real People, gave to their trails and waysides, the stories they told that anchored them to their landscape. I can imagine even less of these stories than I can of Dead Steer or Russian Road, I recognize only a word or two of Nez Perce, and I wonder, without this knowledge, how deep a connection I can ever feel with the Palouse.

But for now, for a little while, I can forget about past and future. I'm living in an illusion, brought about in part by years of living according to an academic calendar, where the year ends in August and begins again in September. Now is time to draw a breath.

The family that is gathered in my kitchen this afternoon is not exactly nuclear. Five women, ranging in age from me at the sink to three-month-old Ali watching from a countertop in her infant seat. My daughter Elizabeth, mother of Ali, presides over the current task. My teenaged daughters, Rachel and Misty, have crowded up on either side to get a good view.

"You hold his scruff and his front feet," Elizabeth had directed me an hour ago as, kneeling on the bathroom floor, she prepared an injection of ketamine for Misty's young cat. "I'll hold his hind feet. But these injections sting, and he'll struggle and try to bite, so be sure you've got a good grip on him."

"What's in that shot?" Misty had wanted to know.

The daughters in summer: Misty (left) and Rachel (right).

"It'll put him to sleep," Elizabeth explained. "Actually it's a dissociative drug. It's sold on the street as vitamin K. He'll be dreaming about flying rainbow-colored mice."

Misty doesn't think the flying mice are funny. She's been dubious about this procedure from the beginning. Now, with her precious white cat unconscious on the kitchen counter, looking as limp as if he were boneless, with his eyes wide open and as unseeing as green stones, Misty is distinctly uneasy. If she could stop things from happening, she would.

Elizabeth washes the cat's hinder parts with liquid hand soap, rinses him off with rubbing alcohol. Peels the paper wrapper from her disposable blade. As the girls bend closer to watch, she stabs through the tough skin of the cat's scrotum and slices it open.

"*Why?*" Misty had pleaded.

"Because it'll make him a better cat. He won't spray, he won't stray, he won't run the risk of testicular tumors when he gets older—"

Misty asks now, "If cats get testicular tumors, why don't guys get them?"

"They do. They get testicular cancer, they get prostate disease—"

"Then why don't guys get their balls cut off?"

Elizabeth doesn't try to answer that one. She probes with her fingers and draws out the first tiny testicle, like a fat white raisin on the end of two threads. She pulls hard enough on the threads to jiggle the unconscious cat.

"Oh," wails Misty, "I wish his eyes weren't open."

"Here's your anatomy lesson," Elizabeth says. "This cord is the testicular cord, and these are the vessels that the sperm would swim up. After I nip off the testicle, like this"—she looks around for somewhere to dispose of the fleshy fragment, and I hand over the garbage pail from under the sink—"then you tie the cords together in a knot, like this"— she makes three quick hard knots, as though she were tying a child's shoestring—"and then the other testicle."

Yank, snip, knot.

"Now we just shake the cords back inside the scrotum, like this, and we're all done."

Not counting the hour we waited until the anaesthetic took effect, the neutering has taken less than ten minutes, and Elizabeth has saved Misty a fifty-dollar vet bill. Now she sponges the minute bloodstains off the cat's white fur and goes to the sink to wash her hands.

"He'll probably sleep for the rest of the afternoon," she says, as Misty gathers her unseeing cat in her arms and croons to him.

Elizabeth lifts Ali from her baby seat and carries her to the rocking chair to nurse her. She's been grumbling about the weight she hasn't taken off since Ali's birth, but she looks as slim to me as she did when she was Rachel's age. Bird-boned, we said about Elizabeth when she was small, and she still has the long, slender body with the delicate wrists that belie the work she does. Pregnancy-testing buffaloes, palpitating mares, delivering calves and colts and baby llamas—probably the heaviest work she's had to do in the three years she's been a practicing veterinarian is repairing prolapsed uteruses. Where I see the obvious physical change in her is in her hands, which once looked young and boneless and now are brown and supple and strong. Competent hands, perhaps more competent than she quite believes them to be.

Ali's birth brought about a crisis in Elizabeth's employment. The middle-aged male veterinarian she worked for wasn't pleased about her pregnancy. One difficulty between them led to another, and now Elizabeth is working part-time at a small rural clinic about thirty miles from my home. Every week she makes the five-hour drive down from northern Washington with Ali, works for two days, and drives home again, where her husband has been feeding their livestock, working at his own job, and caring for their six-year-old son.

I've been worried about her long-distance driving with the baby, concerned about the stress on her and her family, hoping she doesn't let the actions of her former employer erode her confidence in herself. But Elizabeth is a grown-up, after all, she's thirty-six years old (twenty-one years and one day older than her half-sister, Rachel), she's a good veterinarian, and she looks more relaxed and surer of herself every week, now that she's enjoying her job again. She brings home great stories for us, like the steer she recently brought back from the brink after his owner nearly killed him by feeding him on stale bagels.

"I was getting the bagels free, and I thought they'd be good for the steer," the owner had defended himself. "After all, they're carbohydrates."

Every story in the present tense is a work in progress, and I have no way of knowing how Elizabeth will resolve her difficulties. How she'll settle her impending lawsuit with her former employer, when she'll get her home in northern Washington sold, when she'll be able to buy a clinic and open her own vet-

erinary practice—that page hasn't turned. Then there's her husband's job, what to do with their horses, where they're going to
enroll their son in school in the fall. There's always something.
One crisis settled, a page turned, another crisis.

Ali smacks and gulps at her mother's breast. One small hand
clutches her mother's shirt, one small leg jerks and kicks. She
puts me in mind of a baby lamb butting its mother and jerking
its tail as it nurses. Elizabeth cradles her as she begins to drowse.
Looks up at me.

"You know that that injection I gave Misty's cat probably
cost less than fifty cents," she remarks.

"Oh, you vets!" I tease her. "You make terrible markups."

Elizabeth draws a sharp breath, hurt in her eyes, in the
instant before she picks up on my tone. And I am reminded for
the thousandth time of a mother's power to sting, a power I
never remember I have until I see it reflected in a daughter's
face.

"Can Misty stay with us while her mother's gone?" asks Rachel.
"Her mother has to go into dry-out for two weeks."

Misty. One of Rachel's at-risk friends, as the teachers describe
her. I've seen Misty, she's been in and out of our house several
times. She's a grade ahead of Rachel in junior high, a petite girl
with a cloud of dark hair and a face full of secrets. An aura of
trouble emanates from her, although I won't know all its details
for several more months. *It goes back three generations*, others will
tell me. For now I'm only aware that, whatever disturbance fes-
ters within Misty, Rachel has taken her under her wing. At her
age, Elizabeth brought home stray animals. Rachel brings home
people.

Now the challenge rises like a storm in Rachel's eyes.

"Two weeks," I agree.

So Misty arrives with her backpack and her closed little face.
I offer her the guest bedroom, but she prefers to sleep with
Rachel in Rachel's bed. In fact, when she isn't following Rachel

like a silent shadow, I hardly ever set eyes on Misty, although I am constantly aware of her presence. I tell myself it's like having a terrified strange cat in the house. She seems to lurk and hide and watch, slipping in and out of Rachel's room, responding only to my direct questions—would you like another glass of milk, what time do you have to be at school. Often she cries, but only Rachel knows when or why.

A couple of days after Misty moves in, my doorbell rings, and I find two social workers on the doorstep. Somehow I'm not surprised. I invite the two young women into my living room and watch them as they mentally inventory the scene. Me in my shirt and blue jeans and bare feet. Books and houseplants, my quilting clutter, and my old black cat sleeping in the patch of sunlight that falls through the glass doors from the deck.

"We met another cat on the porch."

"Yes, that was Charles Browning. He came from a friend's woodpile."

Later I'll learn that Misty's social worker, Kim, sees a clear correlation between people who take in cats and people who take in foster children. "We once had a child who was allergic to cats," Kim will explain, "and we could not find a home for her that didn't have a cat. Finally we found a family that agreed to keep their cat outside as long as the little girl stayed with them."

Some might hear Kim's anecdote as trivializing the child and her plight, but I don't; after two years of pondering my own impulses, it seems to me that the decision to shelter a child has less to do with lofty motives than with mush-heartedness. *God, Mary, why?* friends have asked me, and all I can answer is that becoming a foster mother is not a role I would have gone in search of. Misty found Rachel and me, and I couldn't turn my back on her.

But all this is to get ahead of the story. For now, Kim only says, "We understand that you have a houseguest," and I answer, "Yes, Misty's staying with us for a few weeks."

Mary at work on a Double Wedding Ring quilt. A Broken Star hangs behind her.

"Would you consider making it a longer commitment?"

I believe that I raised a token objection or two. I'm a single parent, can single women be foster mothers? *Oh yes, no problem.* I still don't know Misty well, do you know her well? *Yes, very well, and she shows more maturity than the people who are supposed to be the adults in her life—*

Can I think it over?

Certainly.

That was two years ago. Much of what has taken place since then is a story I cannot write. Maybe someday. For now, even to reveal that Misty is a foster child is a breach of her privacy. And yet, how to account for this extra daughter who dances through my house, singing to her cat?

I'm reminded that Misty's genes are not mine when she's not feeling well; I don't sense the rhythms of her body the way I do Rachel's, I can never sense whether Misty's ache or sniffle will go away by itself or develop into something longer-lasting. Misty grew in another woman's womb. Her blood courses from other springs than mine, the experiences of her first sixteen years differ so much from mine that we might have grown up on opposite sides of the earth instead of in contiguous Rocky Mountain states. She's been a nomad of the urban west, the trailer courts and small-town rentals, a few years in Spokane with her mother, a few months down here in the Palouse with her father, a refuge on an aunt's couch, a pad, a split. Hearing of my childhood of four-generation permanence on a Montana ranch, her eyes widen. "You went to a one-room country school? *Really*? With an *outhouse*?"

Foster children can break hearts. Unwilling to accept alien love, they are likely to pick quarrels with their foster parents as they near their eighteenth birthdays. They'd rather leave in anger than in pain, Misty's social worker explains, and they are drawn back to the springs of their births. Just last year, Misty's own brother turned eighteen, left the family that had bent over backwards for him, and went back to live with his mother and her boyfriend—but that's another story I'm not at liberty to tell.

What will Misty choose? The page hasn't turned. But she sleeps in her own room now, she's brought her high school grades up to mostly As, and she's working two jobs and saving for a car. Right now she's nut-brown from a summer of river beaches and volleyball in the park, although I don't know how she finds time in the sun between her weekend shifts at Safeway and her nine-to-five job at the county animal shelter, which accounts for the new dog at our house.

A Rottweiler? Oh, Misty!

But she's so sweet! You'll see, Mary, you'll love her.

We've fallen into a summer routine. Elizabeth arrives late on a Tuesday night, nurses Ali until she falls asleep, then visits with me until she can relax from her five-hour drive and go to bed herself. On Wednesday and Thursday mornings, Elizabeth is the first one up. She showers, nurses Ali, and wakes up Rachel to take care of the baby for the day. On her way out the door, she usually passes Misty, headed blear-eyed for the shower. By the time Misty leaves for another day of cleaning cat cages and walking dogs, I've dragged myself out to brew coffee and quilt until I can face another writing day. There's laundry to do, weeding to do. Later I'll shop and make dinner for all of us.

Ali lies on her back on the living room floor, watching the patterns of light and shadow that the leaves cast through the window. She seems excited at the constant flicker and dance. Her mouth falls open, she waves her arms and kicks.

"What are you thinking about?" Rachel asks her.

Ali's eyes wander from the light. She finds Rachel's face, seems to recognize her, and breaks out in a wide, wet baby grin. Rachel leans over her and shakes her hair at her, and Ali coos and makes a random pass at Rachel's hair. She clenches a strand in one tiny fist.

"Ow! Ow! Ow!" says Rachel, pretending to break free, and Ali hangs on and laughs out loud.

Today it's going well, but yesterday Ali cried all morning. Rachel changed her diaper, offered her formula, tried rocking her, tried walking her, but nothing helped. Rachel herself was in tears.

"Tell Elizabeth I won't babysit any longer!" she sobbed, when I came out of my study to see what was wrong. "I've walked her until my arm's tired, but she won't stop crying, she won't take her bottle, she won't go to sleep, and I can't even take a shower, I look like *crap*, because I'm tied to this little *thing*—"

"Give her to me," I said, "and you go and take your shower."

Exhausted from her struggle, Ali fell asleep in my arms. After a while Rachel emerged from the bathroom with wet hair, looking troubled.

"What did you do to get her to sleep?"

"Nothing that you didn't do."

Rachel at fifteen is the tallest of the women in this household. She has inherited her father's athletic strength and his blue eyes, and she would have his heavy fair hair, too, if for reasons of her own she hadn't dyed it dark red this summer. She's self-conscious about her body, but in other respects she's confident, comfortable with herself. Nobody messes with her. "If only I'd been more like her at that age," laments Elizabeth, who was picked on in junior high school. Meanwhile she nearly drives me crazy. *No*, I won't sign a permission slip for her to get a tattoo. *No*, I won't let her get her nose pierced—"Or I'll get a bullhook and lead you around by it," I threaten, and she looks blank, she's never seen anyone leading a bull by the ring in his nose. What her father would think if he had lived to see her at this age, I can't imagine.

And yet Rachel is competent, she's level-headed—*and if I can just get you girls up Fool's Hill*, as my grandmother used to say to my mother and my aunts, enraging them every time she said it.

By that afternoon, Rachel had calmed down. She sat with Ali in her arms, giving her her bottle, and I remarked on how well she was doing. Taking care of a tiny baby wasn't easy, especially for a ten-hour day. Anyone would feel frustrated.

She was listening.

"And you think terrible thoughts—thoughts that you had no idea you could think about a baby—"

One corner of her mouth dragged into a reluctant, inward smile. She lifted Ali carefully on her shoulder and patted a burp out of her.

I see Ali's fist with its strand of Rachel's dark red hair and wonder what that small hand will grow up to hold. What Ali will have to deal with, what she'll live to see. Whether she's the one who will look at me in my dotage and have to decide that the old woman's got to go. As everyone has been telling Rachel lately, who would want to be a parent?

Somewhere on the Palouse is a spring of water that I have never seen. I imagine that it gushes a stream down one of these gullies in the spring, but dries to a mere trickle in summer. Even in July, however, you can guess at its location by the deeper green of grass and the overhanging locust leaves, maybe even by the weight of apples on a tree planted by the white settler who chose the site for his farm because of the spring. I know about the white settler because his great-grandson wrote an essay for a class of mine. *Describe a place that holds significance for you,* had been the assignment that I gave, *and narrate some of its history.*

I think about my daughters. Elizabeth, who remembers my father and the old ways on the ranch. Rachel, who has lived her life so far in university towns, who has traveled with me to England and Finland, but who cares little for the past. Misty, whose life has been impoverished in so many ways, but whose experiences range beyond mine in so many other ways. About Ali's life, who can speculate? But I would wish for all of them the knowledge of the hidden spring. The tree falls in the forest, the clock ticks in the empty room, and we listen, we count the moments. This summer stretches for a few more days, Rachel rocks Ali in her arms, Misty sings in the mornings. Elizabeth holds the lives of the voiceless in her hands. I will write this book.

Selected Bibliography

Alderson, Nannie T., and Helena Huntington Smith. *A Bride Goes West.*
Lincoln: University of Nebraska Press, 1969.

Alexie, Sherman. *The Business of Fancydancing.* Brooklyn, New York:
Hanging Loose Press, 1992.

Ambrose, Stephen E. *Undaunted Courage: Meriwether Lewis, Thomas
Jefferson, and the Opening of the American West.* New York: Simon
and Schuster, 1996.

Anonymous. Unsigned review of *Chip of the Flying U.* Brooklyn Eagle,
1906.

Anonymous. Unsigned letter concerning *Chip of the Flying U,*
Adventure Magazine, 10 December 1924.

Ardinger, Rick. *Goodbye, Magpie.* Boise, Idaho: Floating Ink Books, 1995.

Armitage, Susan, and Elizabeth Jameson. *The Women's West.* Norman:
University of Oklahoma Press, 1987.

Barnes, Kim. *In the Wilderness.* New York: Doubleday, 1996.

Barnes, Kim, and Mary Clearman Blew, eds. *Circle of Women: An
Anthology of Contemporary Western Women's Writing.* New York:
Penguin, 1994.

Berger, Clemence Gourneau. "Metis Come to Judith Basin." *The Metis
Centennial Celebration Publication,* ed. William W. Thackeray, Jr.
Lewistown, Montana, 1979.

Bevis, William W. *Ten Tough Trips: Montana Literature and the West.*
Seattle: University of Washington Press, 1990.

Birkets, Sven. "The Narrowing Ledge." *Associated Writing Programs
Chronicle* 27, no. 1 (1998), 23.

Blew, Mary Clearman. *All but the Waltz: Essays on a Montana Family*.
    New York: Viking, 1991.
Bower, B. M. *Chip of the Flying U*. New York: G. W. Dillingham, 1906.
    Reprint. Lincoln: University of Nebraska Press, 1995.
Bowers, Janice E. *Fear Falls Away*. Tucson: University of Arizona Press,
    1997.
Brink, Carol Ryrie. *Buffalo Coat*. New York: Macmillan, 1944. Reprint.
    Pullman: Washington State University Press, 1993.
————. *Strangers in the Forest*. New York: Macmillan, 1959. Reprint.
    Pullman: Washington State University Press, 1993.
————. *Snow in the River*. New York: Macmillan, 1964. Reprint.
    Pullman: Washington State University Press, 1993.
Brown, Annora. *Old Man's Garden*. Sidney, British Columbia: Gray's
    Publishing, 1954.
Churchward, James. *The Lost Continent of Mu*. Mount Vernon, New
    York: James Churchward, 1933.
————. *Cosmic Forces as They Were Taught in Mu*. Mount Vernon, New
    York: James Churchward, 1926.
Coues, Elliott, ed. *History of the Expedition under the Command of Lewis
    and Clark*. Reprint. New York: Dover, n.d.
Cowan, Emma Carpenter. "A Trip to the National Park in 1877."
    Reprinted in *The Last Best Place*, William Kittredge and Annick
    Smith, eds. Helena: Montana Historical Society Press, 1988.
Cundy, Harold J. Unpublished manuscript. Tacoma: Washington State
    Historical Society, ca. 1939.
Doig, Ivan. *English Creek*. New York: Atheneum, 1984.
Engin, Orrin A. *Writer of the Plains: The Biography of B. M. Bower*.
    Culver City, California: Pontine Press, 1973.
Entrikin, J. Nicholas. *The Betweenness of Place: Towards a Geography of
    Modernity*. Baltimore: Johns Hopkins Press, 1991.
Evans, Steven Ross. *Voice of the Old Wolf: Lucullus Virgil McWhorter and
    the Nez Perce Indians*. Pullman: Washington State University Press,
    1996.
Fergus County Argus, 6, no. 47 (Lewistown, Fergus County, Montana
    Territory, Thursday, June 20, 1889), 2.
————, 6, no. 48 (Lewistown, Fergus County, Montana Territory,
    Thursday, June 27, 1889), 3.
— ————, 6, no. 51 (Lewistown, Fergus County, Montana Territory, July
    18, 1889), 2.
Fiedler, Leslie. "Montana: Or the End of Jean Jacques Rousseau."
    Partisan Review 16 (December 1949), 1239–1248.

Garcia, Andrew. *Tough Trip through Paradise*. Bennett Stein, ed. Sausalito, California: Comstock, 1967.

Gloss, Molly. *The Jump-Off Creek*. Boston: Houghton Mifflin, 1989.

Guthrie, A. B., Jr. *The Big Sky*. Boston: Houghton Mifflin, 1947.

————. *The Way West*. Boston: Houghton Mifflin, 1950.

————. *These Thousand Hills*. Boston: Houghton Mifflin, 1956.

————. *Arfive*. Boston: Houghton Mifflin, 1970.

————. *The Last Valley*. Boston: Houghton Mifflin, 1975.

Hale, Janet Campbell. *Bloodlines*. New York: Random House, 1993.

Hamilton, Ladd. *This Bloody Deed: The Magruder Incident*. Pullman: Washington State University Press, 1995.

————. *Snowbound*. Pullman: Washington State University Press, 1997.

Hansen, Ron. *Nebraska*. New York: Atlantic Monthly Press, 1989.

Hardeman, Nicholas P. "Brick Stronghold of the Border: Fort Assinniboine 1879–1911." *Montana The Magazine of Western History* 29 (1979), 54–67.

Heilbrun, Carolyn G. *Writing a Woman's Life*. New York: Ballantine, 1988.

Hogeland, Abraham. Unpublished notes in author's possession.

Hogeland, Frank W. "Hogelands in Montana." In "Abraham and Mary Hogeland and Descendants," R. H. Murray, ed. Unpublished manuscript in author's possession.

Houston, Pam. *Cowboys Are My Weakness*. New York: W. W. Norton, 1992.

Howard, Joseph Kinsey. *Montana: High, Wide and Handsome*. New Haven: Yale University Press, 1943.

————. *Montana Margins*. New Haven: Yale University Press, 1946.

————. *Strange Empire*. New York: William Morrow, 1952.

Johnson, Dorothy. *Indian Country*. New York: Ballantine, 1953.

————. *The Hanging Tree*. New York: Ballantine, 1957.

————. *A Man Called Horse and Other Stories*. New York: Ballantine, 1957.

————. *When You and I Were Young, Whitefish*. Missoula, Montana: Mountain Press, 1982.

Jordan, Teresa. *Riding the White Horse Home*. New York: Pantheon, 1993.

Keyser, James D. *Indian Rock Art of the Columbia Plateau*. Seattle: University of Washington Press, 1992.

Kittredge, William. *Owning It All*. St. Paul: Graywolf Press, 1987.

————. *Hole in the Sky: A Memoir*. New York: Alfred A. Knopf, 1992.

Lang, William W. "Centennial Biographies: Charles A. Broadwater and the Main Chance in Montana." *Montana The Magazine of Western History* 39, no. 3 (Summer 1989): 30–41.

———. "Lewis and Clark on the Columbia River: The Power of Landscape in the Exploration Experience." *Pacific Northwest Quarterly* 87, no. 3 (Summer 1996): 141–148.

Lavender, David. *Let Me Be Free: The Nez Perce Tragedy*. New York: HarperCollins, 1992.

Layman, William D. "Drawing with Vision: Harold J. Cundy's Pioneering Investigations into the Rock Art of North Central Washington." *Columbia: The Magazine of Northwest History* 12, no. 1 (Spring 1998): 23–31.

Lewistown Daily News, no. 214, Special 75-Year Edition (Lewistown, Montana, Friday, February 7, 1958), 6.

Limerick, Patricia Nelson. *The Legacy of Conquest: The Unbroken Past of the American West*. New York: W. W. Norton, 1987.

Lowell, Robert. *Near the Ocean*. London: Farrar and Farrar, 1967.

Malone, Michael P., Richard B. Roeder, and William L. Lang. *Montana: A History of Two Centuries*. Rev. ed. Seattle: University of Washington Press, 1991.

McLaughlin, Ruth. "Seasons." In *Best American Short Stories*, Joyce Carol Oates, ed. Boston: Houghton Mifflin, 1979.

McNickle, D'Arcy. *The Surrounded*. New York: Dodd, Mead, 1936. Reprint. Albuquerque: University of New Mexico Press, 1988.

McWhorter, Lucullus Virgil. *Yellow Wolf: His Own Story*. Caldwell, Idaho: Caxton Press, 1940.

Messer, Neidy. *In Far Corners*. Lewiston, Idaho: Confluence Press, 1990.

Morris, Gregory L. *Talking Up a Storm: Voices of the New West*. Lincoln: University of Nebraska Press, 1994.

Mourning Dove. "A Mix-Up at Picture Rocks." Unpublished story told to Harold J. Cundy ca. 1934 and quoted in his manuscript of ca. 1939. Tacoma: Washington State Historical Society.

Olsen, Brett J. "Wallace Stegner and the Environmental Ethic: Environmentalism as a Rejection of Western Myth." *Western American Literature* 24, no. 2 (August 1994): 133–134.

Rember, John. "On Going Back to Sawtooth Valley." In *Where the Morning Light's Still Blue*, William Studebaker and Rick Ardinger, eds. Moscow: University of Idaho Press, 1994.

Schemm, Mildred Walker. "The Major's Lady: Natawista." *Montana Magazine of History* 2, no. 1 (January 1952): 5–16.

Schemm, Ripley. "Songs Were Horses I Rode." In *Mapping My Father*. Story, Wyoming: Dooryard Press, 1981.

Sky, Gino. *Appaloosa Rising*. New York: Doubleday, 1980.

Smith, Annick. "It's Come to This." In *Best American Short Stories*, Robert Stone, ed. Boston: Houghton Mifflin, 1992.

————. *Homestead*. Minneapolis: Milkweed Editions, 1995.
Smith, Steve. *The Years and the Wind and the Rain: A Biography of Dorothy M. Johnson*. Missoula, Montana: Pictorial Histories Publishing Company, 1984.
Stegner, Wallace. *Where the Bluebird Sings to the Lemonade Springs: Living and Writing in the West*. New York: Penguin, 1992.
Studebaker, William. *The Rat Lady at the Company Dump*. Boise, Idaho: Limberlost Press, 1990.
Taylor, J. M., R. M. Myers, and I. N. M. Wainwright. "Scientific Studies of Indian Rock Paintings in Canada." *Bulletin of the American Institute for Conservation* 12, no. 2 (1974): 28–43.
Tuan, Yi-fu. *Topophilia: A Study of Environmental Perception, Attitudes, and Values*. Englewood Cliffs, New Jersey: Prentice-Hall, 1974.
Turner, Frederick Jackson. *The Early Writings of Frederick Jackson Turner*. Everett E. Edwards, ed. Madison: University of Wisconsin Press, 1938.
Tuska, Jon. *The West in Fiction*. Lincoln: University of Nebraska Press, 1988.
Ude, Wayne. *Becoming Coyote*. Amherst, Massachusetts: Lynx House Press, 1981.
Walker, Mildred. *Winter Wheat*. New York: Harcourt, Brace, 1944. Reprint. Lincoln: University of Nebraska Press, 1992.
————. *The Curlew's Cry*. New York: Harcourt, Brace, 1955. Reprint. Lincoln: University of Nebraska Press, 1994.
————. *If a Lion Could Talk*. New York: Harcourt, Brace, 1970. Reprint. Lincoln: University of Nebraska Press, 1995.
Welch, James. *Fools Crow*. New York: Viking Penguin, 1986.
————. *The Indian Lawyer*. New York: W. W. Norton, 1990.
Whiteman, Roberta Hill. *Star Quilt*. Minneapolis, Minnesota: Holy Cow! Press, 1984.
Williamson, Alan. *Pity the Monsters*. New Haven: Yale University Press, 1974.
Wilson, Gary A. *Honky-Tonk Town: Havre's Bootlegging Days*. Helena: Montana Magazine, 1985.
Wister, Owen. *The Virginian*. 1902. Reprint. New York: Penguin, 1979.
Wright, Fay. *Out of Season*. Lewiston, Idaho: Confluence Press, 1981.
Wrigley, Robert. *In the Bank of Beautiful Sins*. New York: Penguin, 1995.
Wyndham, Harald. *Pebble Creek*. Lewiston, Idaho: Confluence Press, 1978.